Biography Today

Profiles of People of Interest to Young Readers

Volume 13
Issue 1
January 2004

Cherie D. Abbey
Managing Editor

Kevin Hillstrom
Editor

Omnigraphics

615 Griswold Street
Detroit, Michigan 48226

Cherie D. Abbey, *Managing Editor*
Kevin Hillstrom, *Editor*

Sheila Fitzgerald, Kevin Hile, Diane Telgen,
and Sue Ellen Thompson, *Staff Writers*

Barry Puckett, *Research Associate*

Allison A. Beckett and Linda Strand, *Research Assistants*

Omnigraphics, Inc.

* * *

Matthew P. Barbour, *Senior Vice President*
Kay Gill, *Vice President — Directories*
Kevin Hayes, *Operations Manager*
Leif Gruenberg, *Development Manager*
David P. Bianco, *Marketing Consultant*

* * *

Peter E. Ruffner, *Publisher*
Frederick G. Ruffner, Jr., *Chairman*

Copyright © 2004 Omnigraphics, Inc.
ISSN 1058-2347 • ISBN 0-7808-0681-6

The information in this publication was compiled from the sources cited and from other sources considered reliable. While every possible effort has been made to ensure reliability, the publisher will not assume liability for damages caused by inaccuracies in the data, and makes no warranty, express or implied, on the accuracy of the information contained herein.

This book is printed on acid-free paper meeting the ANSI Z39.48 Standard. The infinity symbol that appears above indicates that the paper in this book meets that standard.

Printed in the United States

INDEXED IN
Children's Magazine Guide

Contents

Preface

Biography Today is a magazine designed and written for the young reader—ages 9 and above—and covers individuals that librarians and teachers tell us that young people want to know about most: entertainers, athletes, writers, illustrators, cartoonists, and political leaders.

The Plan of the Work

The publication was especially created to appeal to young readers in a format they can enjoy reading and readily understand. Each issue contains approximately 10 sketches arranged alphabetically. Each entry provides at least one picture of the individual profiled, and bold-faced rubrics lead the reader to information on birth, youth, early memories, education, first jobs, marriage and family, career highlights, memorable experiences, hobbies, and honors and awards. Each of the entries ends with a list of easily accessible sources designed to lead the student to further reading on the individual and a current address. Obituary entries are also included, written to provide a perspective on the individual's entire career. Obituaries are clearly marked in both the table of contents and at the beginning of the entry.

Biographies are prepared by Omnigraphics editors after extensive research, utilizing the most current materials available. Those sources that are generally available to students appear in the list of further reading at the end of the sketch.

Indexes

A new index now appears in all *Biography Today* publications. In an effort to make the index easier to use, we have combined the **Name** and **General Index** into one, called the **Cumulative Index**. This new index contains the names of all individuals who have appeared in *Biography Today* since the series began. The names appear in bold faced type, followed by the issue in which they appeared. The General Index also contains the occupations, nationalities, and ethnic and minority origins of individuals profiled. The General Index is cumulative, including references to all individuals who have appeared in the *Biography Today* General Series and the *Biography Today* Special Subject volumes since the series began in 1992.

In a further effort to consolidate and save space, the Birthday and Places of Birth Indexes will be appearing only in the September issue and in the Annual Cumulation.

Our Advisors

This series was reviewed by an Advisory Board comprised of librarians, children's literature specialists, and reading instructors to ensure that the concept of this publication — to provide a readable and accessible biographical magazine for young readers — was on target. They evaluated the title as it developed, and their suggestions have proved invaluable. Any errors, however, are ours alone. We'd like to list the Advisory Board members, and to thank them for their efforts.

Sandra Arden, *Retired*
Assistant Director
Troy Public Library, Troy, MI

Gail Beaver
University of Michigan School of
Information
Ann Arbor, MI

Marilyn Bethel, *Retired*
Broward County Public Library System
Fort Lauderdale, FL

Nancy Bryant
Brookside School Library,
Cranbrook Educational Community
Bloomfield Hills, MI

Cindy Cares
Southfield Public Library
Southfield, MI

Linda Carpino
Detroit Public Library
Detroit, MI

Carol Doll
Wayne State University Library and
Information Science Program
Detroit, MI

Helen Gregory
Grosse Pointe Public Library
Grosse Pointe, MI

Jane Klasing, *Retired*
School Board of Broward County
Fort Lauderdale, FL

Marlene Lee
Broward County Public Library System
Fort Lauderdale, FL

Sylvia Mavrogenes
Miami-Dade Public Library System
Miami, FL

Carole J. McCollough
Detroit, MI

Rosemary Orlando
St. Clair Shores Public Library
St. Clair Shores, MI

Renee Schwartz
Broward County Public Library System
Fort Lauderdale, FL

Lee Sprince
Broward West Regional Library
Fort Lauderdale, FL

Susan Stewart, *Retired*
Birney Middle School Reading
Laboratory, Southfield, MI

Ethel Stoloff, *Retired*
Birney Middle School Library
Southfield, MI

Our Advisory Board stressed to us that we should not shy away from controversial or unconventional people in our profiles, and we have tried to follow their advice. The Advisory Board also mentioned that the sketches might be useful in reluctant reader and adult literacy programs, and we would value any comments librarians might have about the suitability of our magazine for those purposes.

Your Comments Are Welcome

Our goal is to be accurate and up-to-date, to give young readers information they can learn from and enjoy. Now we want to know what you think. Take a look at this issue of *Biography Today*, on approval. Write or call me with your comments. We want to provide an excellent source of biographical information for young people. Let us know how you think we're doing.

Cherie Abbey
Managing Editor, *Biography Today*
Omnigraphics, Inc.
615 Griswold Street
Detroit, MI 48226

editor@biographytoday.com
www.biographytoday.com

Congratulations!

Congratulations to the following individuals and libraries, who are receiving a free copy of *Biography Today*, Vol. 13, No. 1 for suggesting people who appear in this issue:

Kay Altland, York, PA
Miranda Becker, Danville, IL
Amanda Bents, Bonifay, FL
Kylie Blackburn, Parsons, KS
Tonya Carpenter, Vernon, FL
Priscilla Fernandez, Orlando, FL
Dawn Foster, Elmwood Park, NJ
Beverly Harrington, Chicago, IL
Nichole Jones, Edgewater, CO
Lucille Koors, Indianapolis, IN
Erin Lounsbury, Farmingville, NY
Abigail Nicoloff, Waco, TX
Marissa Rayford, Riverdale, MD
Miranda Trimm, Allegan, MI

Natalie Babbitt 1932-

American Children's Author and Illustrator
Creator of the Children's Classic *Tuck Everlasting*

BIRTH

Natalie Babbitt was born Natalie Zane Moore on July 28, 1932, in Dayton, Ohio. Her father, Ralph Zane Moore, changed jobs frequently but at one point worked as a labor relations specialist for General Motors. Her mother, Genevieve (Converse) Moore, was a college graduate and a talented artist who did not pursue a career after her children were born. Natalie has one sister, Diane, who is two years older.

One of Natalie's ancestors was Zebulon Pike, the explorer who discovered Pike's Peak in Colorado. Others were among the earliest American settlers of Ohio and West Virginia. The town of Zanesville, Ohio is named after a member of her father's family.

YOUTH

Babbitt was born during the Great Depression, a time of economic hardship for many American families following the stock market crash of 1929. Despite the family's economic troubles, however, Genevieve Moore wanted her daughters to have every possible advantage. She took them to the opera, to symphony concerts, and to the theater, and she made sure they received lessons in art, piano, and horseback riding. Her social and economic ambitions for the family were one of the reasons why Ralph Moore changed jobs so frequently, moving his family every few years before finally settling down in Cleveland.

>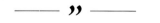
>
> *Babbitt describes herself as a "loner who spent a lot of time drawing and reading, but who liked birthday parties and going to a friend's house after school. A good child who did plenty of bad things. I never got away with anything, though. No matter how clandestine I tried to be, my mother always found me out."*

"There was something indomitable about my parents," Babbitt told an interviewer many years later. "We always managed to have a good time, and my mother saw most of her careful plans for my sister and me come remarkably close to full realization." Genevieve Moore, who had never had a chance to pursue an artistic career herself, decided that Diane would grow up to be a writer and Natalie would be an artist, and she went out of her way to encourage their talents in these directions. She read them all the classic children's books, such as Lewis Carroll's *Alice in Wonderland*, Charles Kingsley's *The Water Babies,* and Booth Tarkington's *Penrod*. Natalie spent much of her time trying to imitate the drawings of glamorous women she'd seen by the Spanish artist Louis de Vargas, who was very popular during the 1940s. By the time she was nine, she decided she wanted to be an illustrator.

Babbitt describes herself as a "fairly average child" who was "by turns confident and scared to death. A loner who spent a lot of time drawing and reading, but who liked birthday parties and going to a friend's house after school. A good child who did plenty of bad things. I never got away with anything, though," she adds. "No matter how clandestine I tried to be, my mother always found me out."

EARLY MEMORIES

When Natalie was less than a year old, her father lost his job and the family had to give up their house. They moved to Indian Lake in northwestern Ohio, where her grandmother owned a cottage. The period during which they lived at the lake had a strong influence on Natalie's later development as a writer and illustrator. Both her grandmother's cottage and the lake itself would reappear in many different forms in her novels. And the heroes and heroines of her books would often be lonely children who had been separated from their homes. Natalie says that as a result of this experience in early childhood, she developed "a deep anxiety about being alone in strange places" that has been with all her life.

EDUCATION

Because her family moved so often, Babbitt attended a number of different elementary schools. As a high school student, she attended the Laurel School for Girls in Shaker Heights, graduating in 1950. She describes herself at Laurel as an underachiever who had little in common with her older sister, a reader of serious literature with a large vocabulary. "She was a straight-A student—a hard and conscientious worker—while I avoided everything that didn't come easily," Natalie admits.

The summer after she graduated from Laurel, Babbitt took a course in fashion illustration at the Cleveland School of Art and decided that she was more interested in creative drawing than in sketching shoes, handbags, and dresses. That fall she began her studies at Smith College, where she majored in art and found herself competing with other students who were just as talented as she was, if not more so. "I had always done what came easily, and what came easily had always been good enough," she recalls. "It was not good enough at Smith, and would never be good enough again."

Although art was her major, Natalie also studied writing at Smith. By that point, she was dating Samuel Babbitt, a student from Yale who wanted to be a novelist. She envisioned a life in which he would write books and she would do illustrations. They were married shortly after her graduation from Smith in 1954.

BECOMING A WRITER AND ILLUSTRATOR

After graduation and marriage, Natalie took a job in the freshman dean's office at Yale University while her husband stayed home and worked on a novel. When he discovered how lonely it was to be a writer and decided to accept a job at Yale as an administrator, she quit her job there and started raising a family.

For the next 10 years Babbitt was busy as a stay-at-home mother and the wife of a college administrator, first at Yale and later at Vanderbilt University in Nashville, Tennessee. Then, in the mid-1960s, when her husband was back at Yale studying for his Ph.D., Natalie had an idea for a children's picture book. She persuaded her husband to write the story while she concentrated on a series of pen-and-ink drawings with contrasting areas of black and white. The result was *The Forty-Ninth Magician,* a story about a young king who promises to look after the sons and grandsons of a court magician who is getting old. Soon after its publication in 1966, Natalie's husband accepted a job as president of Kirkland College in upstate New York, and once he again he put aside the idea of becoming a writer.

After moving to Clinton, New York, where they would live for the next 12 years, Natalie read Betty Friedan's nonfiction work, *The Feminine Mystique.* During the early days of the feminist movement, this influential book inspired many women to develop their talents and pursue their own careers. Although she had been very successful as a homemaker and an academic administrator's wife, she realized that she was not completely happy. "Then Betty Friedan's book came out and I understood why I was so frustrated," she says. She realized that if she wanted to pursue a career as a book illustrator, she would have to write the books herself.

CAREER HIGHLIGHTS

Early Picture Books and *The Search for Delicious*

Babbitt decided to try writing children's books herself. She was encouraged to give it a try by Michael di Capua, the editor at Farrar, Straus, & Giroux who had worked with her husband on his book. Over the next two years, she wrote and illustrated two picture books with stories in rhyming verse. *Dick Foote and the Shark* (1967) tells the tale of a Cape Cod poet in the 19th century who tries to convince his father, a fisherman, that writing poetry is a worthwhile venture. Their difference of opinion is finally resolved when Dick saves himself and his father from a shark attack by reciting a poem. Critics praised the book for its "bouncing rhythms and ingenious rhymes" as well as for its black ink drawings with a sea-green wash.

The SEARCH for DELICIOUS

Natalie Babbitt

By the author of TUCK EVERLASTING

Babbitt's second picture book was *Phoebe's Revolt* (1968), about a turn-of-the-century tomboy named Phoebe who hates the frilly dresses that are the accepted style for girls her age. Her father decides to teach her a lesson by forcing her to wear his clothes for a week. She eventually compromises by agreeing to wear the sailor dresses that her mother has made for her. Babbitt's illustrations for this book showed a more extensive use of shading and a sepia (brownish) wash, which gave the entire book an antique look.

After the success of these picture books for young readers, di Capua urged Babbitt to try writing something longer. The result was *The Search for Delicious* (1969), a novel about a 12-year-old boy named Gaylen and his search for the perfect definition of the word "delicious." Gaylen is the adopted son of the Prime Minister, who is writing a dictionary and can't quite decide on the best definition for this word. So he sends Gaylen on a journey through the kingdom to conduct a national poll on its meaning. During his travels he meets a minstrel named Canto, who gives him the key to an underwater house belonging to a mermaid named Ardis. When Gaylen emerges from his visit to Ardis's underwater world, he does so with a new maturity and sense of his mission in life. It is only then that he can successfully confront Hemlock, the villain of the story, who is trying to hoard the kingdom's water supply. With Ardis's help, Gaylen is able to thwart Hemlock's plan and bring about widespread agreement on the true meaning of the word "delicious."

> *Writing for young people isn't all that different from writing for adults, according to Babbitt. "I believe that children are far more perceptive and wise than American books give them credit for being."*

The Search for Delicious was Babbitt's first work of fantasy. According to *Horn Book,* it showed her willingness to "explore complex themes and ethical dilemmas." The book was also praised by critics for its intricate plot as well as its humor and "haunting language." The *New York Times* selected it as the year's best novel for 9 to 12 year olds.

Myths, Monsters, and Mansions

In the early 1970s Babbitt published four more books for children. *Kneeknock Rise* (1970) tells the story of a young boy, Egan, who visits relatives in the small town of Instep, located at the foot of a small mountain called Kneeknock Rise that is home to a mythical monster called the Megrimum.

One of Egan's uncles has disappeared and may have been captured by the Megrimum. When Egan and his dog climb Kneeknock Rise to search for his Uncle Ott, they discover that there is a perfectly logical explanation for the moaning sound that people have heard coming from the mountain. But the inhabitants of Instep would rather hold on to their illusions than give up their village's only claim to fame. *Kneeknock Rise* was a John Newbery Honor Book and was cited as a Notable Book by the American Library Association.

The Something (1970) is a picture book for young readers that was inspired by Babbitt's own fear of the dark when she was a child. Its hero is Mylo, a troll-like child with buck teeth, skinny arms and legs, and a fur-covered body who is terrified of the "something" that lurks in the dark. He finally comes to terms with his fear by making a statue of "The Something" from the clay that his mother has bought him. Babbitt's illustrations for this book are more cartoon-like and have more shading than those created for her earlier picture books. The overall effect is darker, making Mylo's fears easy to imagine.

The mystery *Goody Hall* (1971) was inspired largely by Babbitt's memories of her own mother, who died when Babbitt was only 24 and who had dedicated her life to the pursuit of wealth and social acceptability. Goody Hall is a Victorian mansion where Mrs. Goody lives with her son, Willet. Her husband, a wealthy miser named Midas Goody, has disappeared, prompting Hercules Feltwright, her son's tutor, to investigate. The story has many parallels to the myth of Hercules, who performed 12 difficult "labors" or tasks and became a god after his death, as well as references to the story of the mythical King Midas, who had the power of turning everything he touched into gold. Although some critics found the book's happy ending too contrived, others praised its "high-spirited, hugely complicated plot."

Babbitt followed that up with *The Devil's Storybook* in 1974. This collection of ten short stores is about a devil who tries to lure more people to Hell but usually ends up being tricked. It revealed Babbitt's skill in writing traditional tales and led to the 1987 sequel, *The Devil's Other Storybook,* 13 years later.

Babbitt's Masterpiece: *Tuck Everlasting*

With three picture books, three novels, and a volume of short stories behind her, Babbitt was ready to combine her interest in fantasy, folk tale, and mythology in *Tuck Everlasting* (1975), the book for which she would become famous. It takes place in the late 19th century in a place that recalls both Babbitt's grandmother's lakefront cottage in Ohio and the Adirondack Mountains, where Babbitt was living when she wrote the book. Winnie Foster, the heroine of the story, is a 10-year-old girl who lives a very protected, orderly life until the day she decides to explore the woods surrounding her fenced-in yard. There she discovers a spring that bubbles up from the trunk of an old oak tree. She is about to drink from it when she is stopped by Jessie Tuck, a 17-year-old boy who explains that whoever drinks the water will become immortal. He and his family — his parents Angus and Mae Tuck and his brother, Miles — took a drink from the spring 87 years ago and are now trapped in the bodies they will inhabit forever.

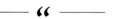

> *Babbitt remains bothered by the fact that so many students are being forced to read her book.* "Tuck *is not a crowd-pleaser," she said. "But it has apparently come to seem useful, particularly for classroom discussions about death — though that is not, to my mind, its central theme." She often says that she would rather have children "examine their own reactions to it as a piece of fiction, and not simply talk about whether they would like to live forever or not."*

The Tucks kidnap Winnie to ensure that she keeps their secret. The villain of the story, referred to only as "the man in the yellow suit," witnesses her kidnaping and offers her parents a trade: he will rescue their daughter if they will turn over ownership of the woods. He has heard rumors about the Tucks and their magical spring, and he is obsessed with finding them so that he can bottle the water and sell it. He tries to force Winnie to drink from the spring, but Mae Tuck steps in. Winnie's efforts to help Mae show that she is mature enough to make decisions for her own future.

Alexis Bledel as Winnie Foster in the movie Tuck Everlasting, *with Amy Irving as her controlling mother and Ben Kingsley as "The Man in the Yellow Suit."*

Because it dealt with such important issues as death, immortality, and change, *Tuck Everlasting* appealed to adult as well as young readers and quickly became a children's classic. It reminded many readers of their favorite fairy tales, and teachers welcomed the book for the lively discussions it provoked about whether or not living forever was really a good thing. Critics compared *Tuck* to other notable children's classics, including E. B. White's *Charlotte's Web*. The International Board on Books for Young People placed Babbitt's book on their honor list, and novelist Anne Tyler, who reviewed the book for the *New York Times,* called *Tuck Everlasting* "one of the best books ever written — for any age."

Tuck Everlasting was later made into a movie starring Alexis Bledel from television's "The Gilmore Girls," as well as Jonathan Jackson, Ben Kingsley, William Hurt, and Sissy Spacek. (For more information on Bledel, see *Biography Today*, Jan. 2003.) The 2002 movie earned mixed reviews. Some critics praised its sensitive handling of deep issues and claimed that it would appeal to a wide audience. "*Tuck Everlasting,* a sweeping romantic fable about love and mortality, targets an audience of girls in their early teens, but has been made with such skill and sensitivity that its appeal spans generations," Kevin Thomas wrote in the *Los Angeles Times.* But other reviewers felt that the movie did a poor job of capturing the magic of the novel. "*Tuck Everlasting* is the softest, sorriest excuse for so-called 'inspirational cinema' that Hollywood has produced this year," wrote Craig Outhier in the *Orange County Register*. "It's overnarrated and underwritten, unimaginatively filmed and inflated with gaseous platitudes that rise, helium-like, into a vast and featureless sky of strained morality."

Despite the success of the novel over the past 25 years, Babbitt remains bothered by the fact that so many students are being forced to read her book. "*Tuck* is not a crowd-pleaser," she said. "But it has apparently come to seem useful, particularly for classroom discussions about death — though that is not, to my mind, its central theme." She often says that she would rather have children "examine their own reactions to it as a piece of fiction, and not simply talk about whether they would like to live forever or not."

The Eyes of the Amaryllis and Herbert Rowbarge

In her subsequent works, Babbitt continued to explore what became one of her favorite themes: people who, like the Tucks, are "frozen in time." Her next book, *The Eyes of the Amaryllis* (1979), tells the story of an old woman on Cape Cod named Geneva Reade, who loses her sea captain husband when his ship, the *Amaryllis,* sinks before her eyes. She spends the next 30 years combing the beach after every high tide, waiting for her husband to send her a sign of his enduring love. Her own son, George, marries and moves inland to escape his mother's obsession, but when Geneva breaks her ankle it is Jenny, George's daughter, who comes to take care of her.

Jenny and Geneva are the only two people who have seen Seward, a ghostly character they meet while beach-combing one evening, who turns out to be the artist who carved the original figurehead for the *Amaryllis*. Seward has struck a bargain with the sea: he will guard the sea's treasures in return for his immortality. When the figurehead washes ashore one day, Geneva quickly seizes it as the sign she has been waiting for, but Seward tries to persuade her to return it because the sea cannot guard the wreck without the figurehead's eyes. A terrible storm erupts, and Geneva almost loses her house and her life as she struggles to hold onto the figurehead that the sea is trying to reclaim. Like *Tuck Everlasting, The Eyes of the Amaryllis* was made into a movie, although it received only lukewarm reviews.

Just as Geneva Reade spends her whole life waiting for a sign from the husband she lost as a young woman, the main character in *Herbert Rowbarge* (1982), Babbitt's next novel, spends his entire life thinking about a twin brother from whom he was separated as a very young child. Herbert and Otto are abandoned as babies and end up in an orphanage. Otto is

adopted soon afterward, while Herbert grows up in the orphanage and never quite recovers from the loss of his twin. He becomes a rich and powerful man who owns a huge amusement park, but even his marriage to a banker's daughter and the birth of his twin girls fail to bring him happiness. The story is told partly from the perspective of the twins, Babe and Louisa, as middle-aged women who must come to terms both with their own long separation from each other and with their father's inability to love them.

Herbert Rowbarge didn't enjoy the same widespread success that *Tuck Everlasting* did. Perhaps this was because the main character is an adult for most of the story and because its style, according to the *New York Times Book Review,* was "so fine and subtle" that only adults could fully appreciate it. Still, it was Babbitt's favorite book up to this point in her career. One reason that she was so attached to the book was that its setting closely resembled the lakefront cottage and town where she and her sister used to spend their summer vacations. "It's about Ohio, where I grew up, and it's about Midwestern things and people," she explained in an interview. "I tried to make it a book for kids, but it did not want to go that way. It's for women over 40."

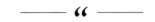

Babbitt's books begin, she says, "with a word or phrase that strikes some kind of sympathetic chord. . . . From this, a group of characters evolves. The characters assume more and more positive personalities, and the events that follow stem from the actions and reactions they might logically be expected to have."

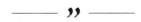

The Valerie Worth Books and More Recent Titles

Early in her career, after her husband abandoned his plans to become a writer, Babbitt had decided that she wouldn't illustrate books that had been written by other people. But she soon dropped that idea and began working with the well-known poet Valerie Worth. In 1972 Worth published a very popular collection called *Small Poems*. Babbitt did a small ink drawing for each poem that captured the subject matter of the poem with great delicacy and accuracy. The result was so successful that she and Worth collaborated on eight more volumes of poems for young readers, which *Booklist* praised for the "small ink drawings [that] embody the realistic and make us imagine much more." Their final joint effort, *Peacock and Other Poems* (2002), was published after Worth's death in 1994. Again the quiet detail of the illustrations earned praise, as Carolyn Phelan wrote in *Booklist*: "Babbitt's precise pencil drawings accompany the

poems, reflecting the words in a quiet and unassuming way."

In addition to illustrating the Valerie Worth poetry books, Babbitt has focused on children's picture books in recent years. *Nellie: A Cat on Her Own* (1989) is about a marionette cat whose creator dies and who must be persuaded that she can still dance without her mistress there to pull the strings. The *Los Angeles Times Book Review* praised Babbitt's watercolor illustrations and called it a book about "the risks and the joys in growing up to be strong and independent." *Bub, or the Very Best Thing* (1994) is a picture book fantasy about a young king and queen who want to find "the very best thing" for their young son, the prince. They look for ideas in books and consult everyone they meet as they walk through the castle grounds. But when they ask the prince himself, he replies "Bub" — a response that the cook's daughter interprets for them as "love." *Elsie Times Eight* (2001) is Babbitt's most recent picture book for children about a fairy godmother who is hard of hearing and has a tendency to misinterpret people's wishes. When Elsie makes a wish, the fairy godmother misunderstands the word "before" and thinks she means there should "be four" Elsies. When Elsie's father shouts, "No! Wait!" she thinks he is saying, "No! Eight" and makes four more Elsies.

Dedicated to Writing for Children

Babbitt says that she is often asked why she doesn't write books for adults. "This question invariably comes from people who do not understand that only in a child's book can a writer take advantage of the widest range of symbolism, express a basic optimism, and have at his disposal the whole vast richness that only fantasy can offer," she explains. She has published numerous essays about literature for children in which she points out that writing for young people isn't all that different from writing for adults. "I believe that children are far more perceptive and wise than American books give them credit for being," she says.

As a result, Babbitt's books never "talk down" to their audiences. In addition to their constant references to folklore, mythology, and classic literature, they treat such complex themes as love, death, immortality, and loyalty. The plots and settings may be fantasy, but the issues they raise are familiar and realistic. At the same time, her books are not filled with as much heroism and violence as most pure fantasy books. They're more likely to focus on a single tragic or violent act and its effect on the rest of the characters.

When she sits down to write, Babbitt always reminds herself, "Don't preach, don't be dishonest, and don't be earnest." Perhaps one of the reasons her books have been so popular with young readers over the years is that they're more interested in telling an entertaining story than in trying to teach a lesson.

Writing Process

Babbitt's books begin, she says, "with a word or phrase that strikes some kind of sympathetic chord. . . . From this, a group of characters evolves. The characters assume more and more positive personalities, and the events that follow stem from the actions and reactions they might logically be expected to have." *Goody Hall*, for example, began with the single word "smuggler."

"I think my writing style and my pictures come out of the same place," Babbitt says. "They're mutually informed by what I see in my head. When you're writing a story, it's like watching a movie—you describe what you're seeing in your head. And illustrating is the same thing—you draw what you see in your head."

MARRIAGE AND FAMILY

Babbitt and her husband, Samuel Fisher Babbitt, have been married since 1954. They have three grown children—Christopher, who is a psychologist; Thomas, who is a composer and rock musician; and Lucy, who is a children's novelist—and three grandchildren. After leaving his posi-

> "
>
> *"I think my writing style and my pictures come out of the same place," Babbitt says. "They're mutually informed by what I see in my head. When you're writing a story, it's like watching a movie— you describe what you're seeing in your head. And illustrating is the same thing— you draw what you see in your head."*
>
> "

tion as president of Kirkland College, Samuel Babbitt became vice president at Brown University. For many years the Babbitts have lived in Providence, Rhode Island, and spent their vacations on Cape Cod.

FAVORITE BOOKS

Babbitt's favorite books are *Alice in Wonderland* and *Through the Looking-Glass* by Lewis Carroll. "These books are full of transformations," she says. "I loved the pig baby and the Cheshire cat and the caterpillar." But she also liked the fact that "Alice wasn't changed at all by her Wonderland experiences. . . . Lewis Carroll didn't want Alice to change. He only wanted to point out, I think, the endless absurdities of the adult world."

SELECTED WRITINGS

As Author and Illustrator

Dick Foote and the Shark, 1967
Phoebe's Revolt, 1968
*The Search for Delicious,*1969
Kneeknock Rise, 1970
The Something, 1970
Goody Hall, 1971
The Devil's Storybook, 1974
Tuck Everlasting, 1975
The Eyes of the Amaryllis, 1977
Herbert Rowbarge, 1982
The Devil's Other Storybook, 1987
Nellie: A Cat on Her Own, 1989
Bub, or The Very Best Thing, 1994
Elsie Times Eight, 2001

As Illustrator

The 49th Magician, 1966
Small Poems, 1972
More Small Poems, 1976
*Still More Small Poems,*1978
Curlicues: The Fortunes of Two Pug Dogs, 1980
Small Poems Again, 1985
Other Small Poems Again, 1986
All the Small Poems, 1987

All the Small Poems and Fourteen More, 1994
Peacock and Other Poems, 2002

SELECTED HONORS AND AWARDS

Best Books of the Year (*The New York Times*): 1969, for *The Search for Delicious;* 1982, for *Herbert Rowbarge*

Notable Children's Books (American Library Association): 1970, for *Kneeknock Rise;* 1974, for *The Devil's Storybook;* 1976, for *Tuck Everlasting;* 1977, for *The Eyes of the Amaryllis;* 1999, for *Ouch! A Tale from Grimm*

Best Book of the Year (*School Library Journal*): 1974, for *The Devil's Storybook*

Christopher Award for Juvenile Fiction: 1976, for *Tuck Everlasting*

Recognition of Merit Award (George C. Stone Center for Children's Books): 1979

Children's Literature Festival Award (Keene State College): 1993

Blue Ribbon Book (*Bulletin of the Center for Children's Books*): 1998, for *Ouch! A Tale from Grimm*

FURTHER READING

Books

Authors and Artists for Young Adults, Vol. 51, 2003
Beacham's Guide to Literature for Young Adults, Vol. 5, 1992
Contemporary Authors New Revision Series, Vol. 38, 1993
Levy, Michael. *Natalie Babbitt,* 1991
Something about the Author, Vol. 106, 1999
Something about the Author Autobiography Series, Vol. 5, 1988
St. James Guide to Children's Writers, 1999

Periodicals

Horn Book, Mar. 2000, p.153
New York Times, Oct. 6, 2000, p.15
New York Times Book Review, Nov. 14, 1982, p.44
Publishers Weekly, Feb. 21, 1994, p.229

Online Databases

Biography Resource Center, 2003, articles from *Authors and Artists for Young Adults,* 2003; *Contemporary Authors Online,* 2001; and *St. James Guide to Children's Writers,* 1999

ADDRESS

Natalie Babbitt
Children's Marketing Department
Farrar, Straus and Giroux
19 Union Square West
New York, NY 10003

WORLD WIDE WEB SITES

http://www.fsgkidsbooks.com
http://www2.scholastic.com
http://www.kidsreads.com/authors/au-babbitt-natalie.asp

David Beckham 1975-

English Soccer Player
Captain of England's National Team, Former Player for
Manchester United, Currently Playing for Real Madrid

BIRTH

David Robert Joseph Beckham was born on May 2, 1975, in
Leytonstone, England. He is the son of Sandra, a hairdresser,
and Ted, a former heating engineer and kitchen renovator who
once played for the local Kingfisher soccer club; Sandra and Ted
Beckham recently divorced. Beckham has two sisters: Lynne,
who is three years older, and Joanne, who is five years younger.

YOUTH

Soccer has dominated Beckham's life since he was a young boy. "All I ever wanted to do was kick a football about," he said, using the European term for soccer. "It didn't enter my head to do anything else. I think I was programmed by my dad to some extent. . . . It wasn't imposed on me, though, and I'm grateful for that." He first started kicking the ball around in his backyard, "but I was murdering the flowerbeds." So he and his friends would go to a nearby park "and just practice and practice for hours on end." By the time he was seven years old, he had started following his father to Wadham Lodge, a small soccer field near their home where he would watch the Kingfishers practice. "It had a little wall all around it and two dugouts. It seemed like a massive stadium to me at the time," Beckham recalled. "I dreamed about playing on that field one day."

"All I ever wanted to do was kick a football about. It didn't enter my head to do anything else. I think I was programmed by my dad to some extent. . . . It wasn't imposed on me, though, and I'm grateful for that."

But Beckham had an even bigger dream than that: he wanted to play for Manchester United, a team that is as famous in England as the New York Yankees are in the United States. In fact, United is considered the most popular sports team in the world, with 53 millions fans. There are fan clubs all over the world, including Africa, New Zealand, Japan, Iceland, and the United States. His father was a huge fan of United, and Beckham has said that this influence was the main factor in his wanting to play there. "I don't know about United born; I was definitely United bred. And what kept me going was the idea that, eventually, I'd get the call I'd been waiting for ever since I'd first kicked a ball."

The Rovers

While he was growing up, Beckham played soccer on multiple teams—on his school teams, on his church team, and also on a youth team called the Ridgeway Rovers beginning at age seven. The Rovers didn't just play in local games, though. The team traveled as far as Germany and Holland, "so we gained the same sort of experience as a professional playing in an international tournament," said Beckham. His father helped with the coaching, and he and other parents became very involved with the Rovers.

This made it a great family experience for the kids during the six years of the team's existence.

When he was ten, Beckham began attending the Bobby Charlton Soccer School each summer. The school ran a well-known skills competition, which Beckham won his second year there. The prize for winning the competition was a training camp trip to Barcelona, Spain. Although he was the youngest player to train at the Barcelona camp and the other players didn't speak English, he found that "if we were playing, we could make ourselves understood. It was the first time I'd been in a professional set-up, training with professional players. It opened my eyes."

EDUCATION

As a student, Beckham wasn't very strong academically, but he loved playing rugby and soccer. He first attended Chase Lane Primary, whose coach made a big impression on him. "I can still remember Mr. McGhee, the teacher who used to coach us: a Scotsman and passionate with it, a bit like [Manchester United coach] Alex Ferguson in fact." In addition to playing for his primary school, Beckham also played for his church's team, the Cubs, "which you could only do if you went to church on Sunday. So all the family . . . made sure we were there every time, without fail."

When he started going to Chingford High, Beckham was disappointed because the school had a rugby team rather than a soccer team. It was coached by a man he admired greatly: John Bullock, whom he described as "tough and disciplined but a lovely man. He was great with all of us and always seemed to have a lot of time for me." Bullock was not interested in soccer, but Beckham and his friends pestered him until the coach agreed to form a school team. "As soon as we had a school soccer team, we started winning leagues and cups, which was great for us. It was great for the school, as well. Maybe the soccer helped me to be happy there. I wasn't that interested in [academic] lessons."

Beckham dropped out of high school in 1991, at age 16, which officially ended his formal education. It was time for him to concentrate on becoming a professional soccer player.

CAREER HIGHLIGHTS

United Trainee

While he was still in school, Beckham had attended a soccer academy run by the Tottenham Hotspurs (known as the Spurs). Tottenham was interested in his potential, but Beckham's favorite team had also taken notice of

Beckham played for Manchester United Youth in 1993,
his last year before turning pro.

the boy. The Spurs soon offered him a six-year contract, which would start with four years in training, followed by two years as a professional. The offer was tempting. But when United laid the same cards on the table, Beckham decided that he would rather play with his favorite team. He signed as a United trainee on July 8, 1991 — the same year that he decided to leave high school.

In European professional soccer, which they call football, many clubs have a farm system, with multiple teams at varying levels of play. When young players like Beckham are signed to a club, they often start their careers by playing on teams at lower levels and then try and work their way up to the top team. In England alone there are 92 teams in four different divisions; the top is Premier, then First, Second, and Third. Manchester United fields a team in the Premier League, the top level. Teams play against other teams in their home country as well as against other teams in Europe and around the world. There are many different tournaments and awards each year. In England, the Premiership is awarded to the champion in the Premier League. The FA Cup, the world's oldest national cup competition, is awarded to the winner of the English Football Association tournament. The champion teams of the various European countries play against each other in an annual tournament whose winner receives the European Cup. Perhaps the most popular and prestigious event is the World Cup, which occurs every four years. It's an elimination-type competition where the number of contenders is reduced through a series of qualifying rounds. Eventually, only two teams are left to play the finals, and then only one team emerges as the winner, the World Cup champion.

When Beckham first started with United, he participated in what is called the Youth Training Scheme (YTS). He remained in this training program for young players while he was getting ready to turn pro. He and his team-mates soon proved their skills when they won the Milk Cup, a tournament in Northern Ireland; in 1992 they won the Football Association's Youth Cup, the first time a United team had done so since 1964. Although they lost the next year, Beckham had convinced United that he was a solid play-er. He was signed to a professional contract on January 22, 1993, though he continued to play on the youth team throughout 1993. His team didn't win the Youth Cup that year, coming in as the runner-up instead. The following year, Beckham played primarily on the United reserve team.

Dreams Come True

For Beckham, playing for Manchester United at their Old Trafford stadium was a dream come true. He began playing for United in 1994, making his debut that September as a substitute in a match against Brighton. Beck-ham could barely realize that he was wearing the jersey for the team of his dreams. "I'd wake up every morning hardly able to believe what was going on around me," he said. "I'd drive into training, thinking to myself: 'I'm a first-team player. I'm doing my work on the main field. . . . I've got my own spot in the car park, with my initials there in white paint.' When I went to the training ground for the first time as a boy, those white lines marked out with the initials of the United players I idolized seemed to represent every-thing I dreamed of achieving for myself. Now, I belonged and it might have been easy to get swept away with it all. People at the club, though, and the manager in particular, didn't let that happen."

―――― " ――――

"[Beckham] is a genius with an innate sense of physics," **Sports Illustrated** *writer Frank Deford once reported. "He has, says one software company, figured out how to balance the kick angle, kick speed, spin, and direction in order to get the optimal turbulent laminar transition trajectory. What trajectory Beckham's brain calculates in seconds from instinct would, engineers say, take computers hours to figure out."*

―――― " ――――

In the 1994-95 season, the United coach eased Beckham into his role on the team at right midfield. He was even loaned out to another team, Preston North End, to gain experi-ence. He played five matches and scored two goals there. He finally made his Premier League debut at home near the end of the season, in April 1995. But things really started to improve for Beckham in the 1995-96 season, when he established himself on the first team. That was also when he first started to show his talent for scoring. United won the Double that year, winning two major tournaments: the FA Cup and the Premiership, the league title.

Beckham started the next season, 1996-97, by scoring his most famous goal. In a game against Wimbledon, the young player proved his remark-able skills by kicking in a goal from 57 yards away—halfway down the soccer field. The stunning play gained him instant fame. His performance that year helped United win the Premiership. In addition, he was named the Professsional Footballers' Association Young Player of the Year.

Beckham was gaining fans, too, who were impressed by his ability to make a soccer ball curve into the net when he kicked it. He is especially good at this when performing a free kick after a penalty. Puzzled by the soccer player's ability, engineers in Japan and Europe have even made it a subject of scientific study. "The conclusion," *Sports Illustrated* writer Frank Deford once reported, "is simply that he is a genius with an innate sense of physics. He has, says one software company, figured out how to balance the kick angle, kick speed, spin, and direction in order to get the optimal turbulent laminar transition trajectory. What trajectory Beckham's brain calculates in seconds from instinct would, engineers say, take computers hours to figure out." His famous kick would later lend itself to the title of a 2002 movie, *Bend It Like Beckham,* about a girl who wants to play soccer as well as her hero.

Recognized Talent Leads to the National Team

The next season, 1997-98, was disappointing for United. They finished second in their league, lost in the FA Cup, and were knocked out of the Champions League quarterfinals. But for Beckham, there was some consolation when he was called up by England's national team. This did

Beckham helped Manchester United win the Premiership in 1997. Here, he celebrates after scoring a goal.

not mean he had to leave his home team, Manchester United. Instead, soccer players who represent their national teams also play for the local teams from which they are selected, like an American professional basketball player would continue to play for their NBA team even when named to the American national team for the Olympics. "It's an honor for any player to represent his country," noted Beckham. "But you can't make it happen for yourself. All you can do is concentrate on playing for your club and hope that you catch the eye of the right person. . . . That first Double-winning season [winning the FA Cup and Premiership], though, brought all of us into the limelight—and into the reckoning as far as England was concerned. When it happened for me, it all came quicker than I could have imagined, and was a bigger thrill than I'd ever let myself dream it might be. Almost overnight, it seemed I went from being a promising player at my club to being a regular part of the England team challenging for a place in the 1998 World Cup in France."

At first, things seemed to be going fine for the England team in 1998. They played well enough to enter the World Cup playoffs. Expectations for Beckham, the team's new rising star, were high. He played as a substitute in a match against Romania; then, in the next game against Colombia, he scored his first goal as an England player. This meant England would make it to the second round, in which they would have to face their archrival, Argentina.

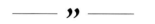

"It's an honor for any player to represent his country," noted Beckham. "But you can't make it happen for yourself. All you can do is concentrate on playing for your club and hope that you catch the eye of the right person. . . . Almost overnight, it seemed I went from being a promising player at my club to being a regular part of the England team challenging for a place in the 1998 World Cup in France."

The Infamous Red Card

England and Argentina had a long history of bitter rivalry, both on the field and off. This dates back to the Falkland Islands War in 1982, when the two nations had clashed over the islands in the south Atlantic off the coast of Argentina. They had even fought a war over it, with Britain coming out the victor. Their hostile feelings were often expressed on the soccer field in intense, aggressive play.

The England players were holding their own against Argentina that June day when a goal set up by Beckham to teammate Michael Owen tied the game at 2-2 at half-time. Early in the second half, though, something happened that would haunt Beckham for years. One of the Argentina players, Diego Simeone, fouled Beckham, and the English player fell to the ground. Beckham described what happened next: "While I was down on the ground, he made as if to ruffle my hair. And gave it a tug. I flicked my leg up backwards towards him. It was instinctive, but the wrong thing to do. You just can't allow yourself to retaliate. I was provoked but, almost at the same moment I reacted, I knew I shouldn't have done. Of course, Simeone went down as if he'd been shot. 'I've made a big mistake here. I'm going to be off.'"

It would prove to be the biggest mistake of Beckham's career. Simeone drew a yellow card (a minor foul), but Beckham was given a red card (a

In this 1998 game between the national teams for England and Argentina, Beckham earned a red card and was ejected from the game. Here, he is sent off by the referee after striking out at Simeone.

major foul) and ejected from the game. England had to play short-handed for 73 minutes and eventually lost in penalty kicks. The match ended in a tie, but England had needed a win to go to the World Cup. Without it, England was out of the competition, and Beckham's major penalty made him the scapegoat. Some of his most loyal fans in Manchester still supported him. But most soccer fans throughout England were outraged and vilified him. The once-adored soccer star was lambasted in the newspapers (one headline read, "What an Idiot!"), was heckled wherever he went, and was even burned in effigy outside one London pub.

The public's scorn even escalated to death threats. Beckham recalled one particularly disturbing occasion: "I received a letter at my house in Worsley that contained two bullets in it and a scrawled note saying there's be one for each of us [him and his wife]. I can still remember standing by my pool table and the sound of the cartridges dropping out of the envelope and onto the table in front of me." Though nothing happened to him, threats such as this are taken very seriously by soccer players like Beckham, who no doubt recall how Colombian player Andres Escobar was murdered after he accidentally lost a World Cup game by kicking the ball into his own team's goal.

Redemption and the 2002 World Cup

Beckham was greatly troubled by the public's reaction to his foul, but he responded by playing some of his best soccer ever. The 1998-99 season proved to be a terrific year, both for Beckham and for Manchester United. Executing fantastic passes and goals, he helped lead United to what is known as the Treble, or Triple Crown. That means the team won three championships: the FA Cup, the English Premiership, and the European Champions Cup, which is considered the ultimate club prize in European soccer. United also won the Inter-Continental Cup in 1999. Also known as the World Club or Toyota Cup, the Inter-Continental Cup is awarded to the winner of a match between the champions of two continents, Europe and South America. The season was the most successful year in the history of the Manchester United club.

The following season, 1999-2000, the team won another English Premier-ship. Beckham was voted second in two competitions, best player in Europe and best player in the world; he lost to Rivaldo of Barcelona and Brazil in both contests. In the 2000-01 season, United again won the English Premiership and Beckham was named Britain's Sportsman of the Year. But his main achievements were in international play. He first captained the England national team in a friendly in Italy (a friendly is an exhibition game). He then kept the captain's armband after that, in World Cup qual-ifying play. In 2001, he led England to a 5-1 win against Germany in a World Cup qualifier. He later shot a last-minute goal on a free kick to win a game against Greece in the final qualifying round. That goal secured England's place in the World Cup finals.

In the World Cup finals, England was slated to play their archrivals, Argen-tina. Beckham was excited but nervous about playing against Argentina, because the humiliation of the 1998 red card incident was still fresh in his memory — and in that of his fans. "I have waited for this game for four years," he said. "I was nervous, but what I had to do was go forward." This game was made even more difficult because he was recovering at that time from an injury to a metatarsal bone in one of his toes — although luckily the injury was to his left foot, not his right or kicking foot.

Beckham knew this was his chance to make things right. The score was tied at 0-0 when he was fouled by an Argentina player. The referee didn't

Beckham scores a goal during the 2002 World Cup match against Argentina.

call it, but that didn't matter because another England player, Michael Owen, was quickly fouled, too. It was time for a penalty kick, and Beckham took the ball. "I remember forcing in two big gulps of air to try and steady myself and take control," he said. "For the last two penalties I'd taken for

United, I'd hit the ball straight down the middle of the goal and the keepers [a line of opponent players protecting the goal], diving to one side, had been nowhere near them. 'Same again now, David.' I was far too nervous to try to be clever. Not nervous for myself any longer. This was all about the team I was captain of. I've never felt such pressure before. I ran forward. And I kicked the ball goalwards as hard as I could. *In.* The roar. *IN!*"

After the kick, Beckham ran directly to the stands filled with Argentine fans, tilted his head back, and roared. England had won it, 1-0. "It's been a long four years. It's been up and down, but this has topped it all off," he later said. "It doesn't get any sweeter than that. As a footballing nation, we have waited a long time for this." In the next round, the quarter-finals, England played against Brazil. Unfortunately, England lost to Brazil, the eventual World Cup winner. But Beckham's redemption was complete.

Popularity

Over the years, Beckham has won a huge fan following. Yet some sports analysts feel that his fan following is not commensurate with his skill and that he is not the most talented player on the field. As British sportswriter Kevin McCarra once put it, "Beckham's talent . . . is deep rather than broad. He is one-paced, cannot trick his way past a fullback, tackles erratically, and has occasionally been faulted for his defensive positioning. All of that has been overshadowed by the precision with which he hits long, diagonal crosses and passes."

Over the past few years, Beckham has become overwhelmingly popular in Britain. Certainly part of his appeal is his physical attractiveness, which cemented his allure to women. Another part is his flashy lifestyle with his wife, Victoria Adams (also known as Posh Spice), a former singer with the Spice Girls. Together, they're the most famous celebrity couple in England. Beckham also has a large following among gay fans, a fact that he embraces: "Being a gay icon is a great honor for me. . . . I'm quite sure of my feminine side, and I've not got a problem with that at all." On the other hand, he sometimes wears gold chains and styles his hair in cornrows, which lends him a certain appeal to black fans. And although he is rich now, his roots are grounded in his blue-collar family background, so he appeals to working-class fans. In this way, Beckham has managed to appeal to all types of people. This has made him a huge asset to his commercial sponsors, which include Adidas, Pepsi, mobile-phone company Vodafone, and Police brand sunglasses. He sometimes models for these companies, and he also has his own clothing design business.

Final Years with Manchester Grow Tense

The first years of the new millennium were good ones for Beckham, or so it seemed. Manchester United had won the English Premiership in 2000 and 2001, though the team had fallen short of the FA Cup and Champions League titles and had won no titles in 2002. The team won the Premiership again to close the 2002-03 season.

But despite such successes, the relationship between Beckham and Alex Ferguson, the coach of Manchester United, was growing increasingly tense. By 2003, Beckham's stardom had become a liability for him professionally. His image as a cultural icon greatly disturbed Coach Ferguson. Especially after Beckham's marriage to Posh Spice, Ferguson felt that his player's mind was not on the game as much as it should be and that he was distracted by such things as photo shoots and family events. Two incidents particularly set Ferguson off: when Beckham missed a practice to be with his son Brooklyn, who was sick, and when he went to Buckingham Palace to meet the queen rather than following orders to take a vacation in order to recuperate from a broken rib.

Beckham's relationship with Ferguson became more and more tense, until it all blew up one day after United lost a game to Arsenal. Ferguson blamed Beckham for the loss, but Beckham felt that the whole team had played

"What happened then doesn't seem real now, thinking back to that afternoon," recalled Beckham. "The boss [Coach Ferguson] took a step or two towards me from the other side of the room. There was a boot on the floor. He swung his leg and kicked it. At me? At the wall? . . . I felt a sting just over my left eye, where the boot had hit me. I put one hand up to it and found myself wiping blood off my eyebrow. I went for the manager. I don't know if I've ever lost control like that in my life before."

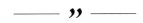

poorly and resented taking all the responsibility. "What happened then doesn't seem real now, thinking back to that afternoon," recalled Beckham. "The boss took a step or two towards me from the other side of the room. There was a boot on the floor. He swung his leg and kicked it. At me? At the wall? . . . I felt a sting just over my left eye, where the boot had hit me. I put one hand up to it and found myself wiping blood off my eyebrow. I went for the manager. I don't know if I've ever lost control like that in my

*Playing for Real Madrid in 2003, Beckham fights off
Santiago Ezquerro Marin of Athletic Bilbao.*

life before." At the end of the 2002-03 season, Beckham was traded and had to leave Manchester United.

Several reasons for the trade have been given, including a desire to change playing tactics and a need to bring in fresh players. This is an issue because Beckham's salary is enough to pay for several less-experienced players. But many observers believe the breakdown in the coach-player relationship was the deciding factor. Knowing that he would be traded, Beckham insisted the only other team he would play for would be Real Madrid, a powerhouse club that had a lot of stars of its own. United agreed, and the Madrid team happily signed him to a six-million-euro-per-year contract, plus bonuses. Having to leave his beloved Manchester United team was a blow for Beckham, but he is still on the England national team as its captain.

Beckham started with Real Madrid in the 2003-04 season. After playing a few games, he finds that he enjoys his new teammates. "This team not only can play great football," he said enthusiastically, "but they can play hard attacking football and they've got a lot of character." Financially, the deal works well for Beckham, too. Not only does he receive an excellent salary from his new team, but some of his major sponsors—Pepsi, Adidas, and Vodafone—are also associated with Real Madrid, so he can continue his sponsorship deals.

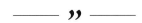

In his ten years of playing professional soccer, Beckham has accomplished a great deal. With the England national team, he earned 60 "caps," meaning 60 appearances in international competition, and scored 11 goals. With Manchester United, he made a total of 394 appearances with the club, scoring 85 goals. As part of United, he helped the team win two FA Cups and six Premierships, plus the European Champions Cup and the Inter-Continental Cup. It's an unprecedented winning streak, comparable to the New York Yankees or the Chicago Bulls.

Beckham started with Real Madrid in the 2003-04 season. After playing a few games, he finds that he enjoys his new teammates. "This team not only can play great football," he said enthusiastically, "but they can play hard attacking football and they've got a lot of character."

Fame has naturally been one consequence of Beckham's success. But while he appreciates the media, he feels they exaggerate his spending habits and desire to be in the spotlight. "None of it is true," he once protested, "and I can't sue or I would end up doing it every day." For Beckham, it really all comes down to one passion: "I have always wanted to be a well-known footballer and all the things that come with it are an amazing bonus. But the important thing for me is to play football."

MARRIAGE AND FAMILY

Beckham was married on July 4, 1999, to pop singer Victoria Adams. His fairy-tale wedding at a romantic Dublin castle was compared with the royal wedding of Charles and Diana. And when Becks and Posh, as they are known in Great Britain, bought a mansion in Hertfordshire, it promptly became known to the English public as "Beckingham Palace" (a play on

Victoria Adams, known as Posh, shows off her diamond solitaire engagement ring in 1998, after she and Beckham announced their plans to marry.

Buckingham Palace, the name of the royal family's home). The Beckhams have two sons: Brooklyn, who was born in 1999 in the New York City borough he was named after, and Romeo, who was born in 2002 and is named after the singer from So Solid Crew.

Beckham is known to be devoted to his family. He even got into trouble with his Manchester United coach because he put his family before soccer. Although Beckham has said that "without my football I'm a lost soul," he has also that "the most important thing to me is my family."

The Beckhams would seem to have it all: money, good looks, and fame. They are certainly idolized for their glamorous lifestyle and commitment to each other and their children. But there is another side to their celebrity lifestyle: the family has received death threats and has been the target of several kidnaping threats. Fortunately, these have all been avoided with the help of the police and increased security measures.

MAJOR INFLUENCES

Other than the early influence of his father, Beckham has found inspiration in his hero Bobby Moore, who is the only captain of an English team to win the World Cup, as well as former England coach Glen Hoddle.

HONORS AND AWARDS

Young Player of the Year (Professional Footballers' Association): 1997
Sir Matt Busby Award: 1997
Player of the Year (Nationwide Football Awards): 2000
Most Valuable Player (Western Union): 2001
Britain's Sportsman of the Year: 2001
BBC Sports Personality of the Year: 2001
Sports Personality of the Year (British Broadcasting Corp.): 2001
Order of the British Empire (Government of Great Britain): 2003

FURTHER READING

Books

Beckham, David. *My World,* 2000
Beckham, David. *Both Feet on the Ground: An Autobiography,* 2003
Newsmakers, Issue 1, 2003
Who's Who in the World, 2001

Periodicals

Economist, July 5, 2003, p.57
Los Angeles Times, Aug. 5, 2001, p.D10
Newsweek, Oct. 16, 2000, p.64
New Statesman, Feb. 10, 2003, p.57
New York Times, July 2, 1998, p.A21
People, May 4, 1998, p.71; June 19, 1999, p.58; June 9, 2003, p.63
Soccer Digest, Aug.-Sep. 2003, p.38
Sporting News, July 7, 2003, p.56
Sports Illustrated, Sep. 7, 1998, p.28; June 23, 2003, p.60
Time, June 30, 2003, p.49
Time International, Apr. 28, 2003, p.65

"I have always wanted to be a well-known footballer and all the things that come with it are an amazing bonus. But the important thing for me is to play football."

Times (London), Mar. 21, 1998, Magazine sec., p.18; Apr. 15, 2000, p.31; Mar. 27, 2001, Sports sec., p.9; June 21, 2001, p.Times2:2; June 2, 2002, Sports sec., p.2; Mar. 27, 2003, p.11; June 19, 2003, p.43; Sep. 17, 2003, Sports sec., p.42; Sep. 14, 2003, Sports sec., p.6
USA Today, June 10, 2002, p.C12
Vanity Fair, Sep. 1999, p.298

Online Databases

Biography Resource Center Online, 2003, article from *Newsmakers,* 2003

ADDRESS

David Beckham
CM Publicity — 19 Management
Unit 32 — Ransomes Dock
35-37 Park Gate Road
London SW11 4NP
UK

WORLD WIDE WEB SITES

http://www.manutd.com
http://www.realmadrid.com

Matel Dawson, Jr. 1921-2002

American Autoworker and Philanthropist

BIRTH

Matel Dawson, Jr., was born on January 3, 1921, in Shreveport, Louisiana. He was the son of Matel Dawson, Sr., a head cook at the Tri-State Sanitarium (now known as the Willis-Knighton Health System) in Shreveport, and Bessie Hall Dawson, a laundress. Dawson was the fifth of their seven children.

YOUTH

Dawson came from a family of humble means, but his parents were proud and hard-working. These were values that they instilled in their son. His father started out as a farmer, growing corn, cotton, and other crops. But tougher times came in the 1930s with the Great Depression. During this period of great economic hardship, many people were out of work and many families were desperately poor. During the Depression, Dawson earned extra income for his growing family by working odd jobs, including work at the state fairgrounds and as a groundskeeper. One of these jobs was being a hospital dishwasher at the Tri-State Sanitarium, and he eventually worked his way up to become head cook. Dawson's mother also earned an income by taking in other people's laundry. Because they worked so hard and remained employed even during the Depression, the family never had to go on welfare, a fact that made Dawson quite proud. "Those were tough times," he said, "but we made it. We were never on welfare and never received any food stamps."

It was Dawson's mother, Bessie, who especially taught him the value of saving. "My mother was a saving woman," he recalled. "Even if it was just two or three dollars, my mother would say 'save.'" As he also humorously noted, she had a way of making a little money stretch a long way: "She could squeeze a buffalo right off a nickel." His mother would always help out neighbors in need, even as her family struggled to get by; and she made her children promise that, when they got older, they would try to "give something back." Dawson would later make good on his promise in a big way.

EARLY MEMORIES

Even though Dawson's family was able to get by financially, living in the South during the 1930s was difficult because it was still a time of very oppressive racism. Many white people felt a deep and abiding prejudice against black people. African-Americans were often treated as inferior, and they were expected to act subservient. At that time, segregation — the separation of African-Americans and whites — was common in the South. The South was still segregated under what were called "Jim Crow" laws. These laws forced the segregation of the races and created "separate but equal" public facilities for blacks and whites in housing, schools, transportation, bathrooms, drinking fountains, and more. Although these separate facilities were called equal, in reality those for blacks were miserably inadequate. African-Americans usually attended dilapidated, impoverished schools with underpaid teachers. After leaving school, their opportunities for work were often just as limited.

This was the society in which Dawson grew up. "Back then," he recalled, "if you were walking down the sidewalk and saw a white person approaching you, you had to get off the sidewalk and let them pass by. We had separate water fountains and always had to ride in the back of the bus." This was a big reason why Dawson later left Shreveport and moved to Detroit. As he put it, "I just thought I'd be more comfortable going somewhere else."

— **"** —

EDUCATION

Dawson's parents only had a seventh-grade education, but, as he said, "they were not illiterate." They valued education, and they made sure their children attended school. Dawson went to West Shreveport Elementary School and Central High School. Unfortunately, because money was so tight, Dawson had to leave school after the ninth grade to earn money and help his family.

"Back then, if you were walking down the sidewalk and saw a white person approaching you, you had to get off the sidewalk and let them pass by," Dawson recalled about growing up in the South. "We had separate water fountains and always had to ride in the back of the bus." This was a big reason why Dawson later left Shreveport and moved to Detroit. As he put it, "I just thought I'd be more comfortable going somewhere else."

CAREER HIGHLIGHTS

Moving to Detroit

Dawson moved to Detroit in 1939. He had two uncles who lived and worked there, and he thought they might help him get a job. It turned out to be a wise decision. His first job was working as a laborer for the Civilian Conservation Corps (CCC). The CCC was a program created by President Franklin D. Roosevelt as part of the "New Deal." These programs helped put unemployed people to work during the Depression. But Dawson only stayed there a few months before one of his uncles, who worked for the Ford Motor Co., was able to get his nephew a job at the River Rouge plant in Dearborn, a suburb of Detroit.

— **"** —

Dawson was hired on September 30, 1940, to work for $1.25 an hour as a steel press operator, an unskilled starting position. But his supervisors soon saw that Dawson was an extremely hard-working and devoted employee,

47

and it wasn't long before he became a forklift driver and rigger—a trade worker who is qualified to perform a number of skilled jobs. Things were soon looking up for Dawson: he had a good, well-paying job, and in 1942 he got married. The couple bought a house, and Dawson worked overtime shifts and weekends to earn extra pay. He would later often say how grateful he was to Ford, which he called "the greatest motor company" for being so progressive in hiring minorities. As he later recalled, "Ford always hired blacks in skill positions, even back then [when I was hired], and they had black supervisors."

> *Dawson would often say how grateful he was to Ford, which he called "the greatest motor company" for being so progressive in hiring minorities. As he later recalled, "Ford always hired blacks in skill positions, even back then [when I was hired], and they had black supervisors."*

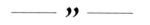

Fortunes Rise and Fall

Then, in 1956, an opportunity came along that Dawson knew he couldn't pass up. Ford offered its employees the option of investing some of their paychecks in stock. "A lot of people didn't want to take it," he recalled. "They thought [stock investment] was just for rich people." But he saw it as a great way to save and earn extra income. Most of the stocks he bought were shares of Ford Motor Co., which over time earned him an average of over 13 percent annually in interest. The money was reinvested in more stock, compounding his interest until his savings really began to grow. But even with putting part of his income into the stock market, Dawson was able to buy a house and pay off its 30-year mortgage in only six years. He also bought a Lincoln Continental for his wife, and a second one for himself.

Things seemed to be going along smoothly for Dawson until 1976, when he suffered through two emotionally traumatic events: his mother died and his wife divorced him. After 35 years of marriage, the divorce came as a particular shock. Not only was it an emotional blow, but it was also a financial blow, as his wife got the house and both cars, as well as half of his investments, in the divorce settlement. Later, he admitted that he had concentrated so much on his work, by often working weekends and never taking a vacation, that he might have neglected his marriage. "I guess I was concentrating on myself too much," he reflected.

Dawson standing in front of a photo and plaque in honor of his parents, Matel Dawson, Sr., and Bessie Hall Dawson.

Charity Becomes the Goal

After the divorce, Dawson gained a new perspective on material possessions and decided they were not so important. He moved into a one-bedroom apartment and for a long time drove a 1985 Ford Escort, which was missing its hubcaps because they had been stolen and he had never bothered to replace them. He realized that doing well for himself and his family wasn't enough and that making contributions to his community would be far more satisfying. So, in the late-1980s, after rebuilding his savings after the divorce, he began to give money to charities—first to his local church, the People's Community Church in Detroit, then to his family's old church in Shreveport. And these weren't $50 or even $100 donations, either, but very sizeable contributions that over a couple years amounted to over $100,000. He also gave money and gifts to members of his family, helping them with house payments and college, though he had always helped them out from the time he had moved to Detroit.

But Dawson wanted to do even more. He remembered how important education had been to his parents, and how he regretted not being able to finish school himself because he had had to work at a young age. So he

49

decided he wanted to help kids get a college education. "We've got to prepare this young generation for the future," he explained. "I choose education because that's the only way we can get things done." So, in 1991, during a fundraising telethon, Dawson made a $30,000 donation to the United Negro College Fund (UNCF). UNCF director Deborah Dolsey Diggs vividly recalled how she met Dawson as he came into the charity's office to give them the check: "He walked into the office in overalls and rubber fisherman's boots up to his knees. In his hand he held a paper bag, and in that bag was a check for $30,000."

Leaving a Legacy

The giving did not stop there, not by any means. Over the years, Dawson donated $240,000 to the UNCF, $632,000 to Wayne State University in Detroit, $300,000 to Louisiana State University in Shreveport, and $150,000 to the National Association for the Advancement of Colored People (NAACP), for a total of $1,322,000. Some of this money went to specific funds. For example, $100,000 went to LSU to establish the Matel and Bessie Hall Dawson Endowed Scholarship Fund named in honor of his parents, and a scholarship fund was also set up in his name at Wayne State University. The scholarships at both universities go to deserving students regardless of race or ethnicity and pay for four years of college. Students who receive the scholarships often are surprised to learn that the money comes not from a rich corporate executive but from a humble forklift operator. Scholarship recipient Sonia Taggart, for example, once said she had assumed that the money came from "someone who would not miss the money he was giving away. Then I found out what he does, where he works, and I think that's what really floors you about him. He's so humble."

Dawson's donation made him a celebrity in Detroit, where he came to be known as the "blue-collar benefactor" and the "forklift philanthropist."

But he didn't donate his money to become famous. In fact, his supervisor at Ford didn't even know that Dawson was donating his money until he heard a story about the forklift operator on the radio. But Dawson did acknowledge that he would like to be remembered for his contributions. As he put it, "I'm not trying to impress anybody. I just want to help people, leave a legacy, and be remembered."

Working until the End

Most people who have led such a successful life would look forward to retirement and resting by the age of 65, but Dawson never had the urge to retire. He worked until the age of 81, getting up at 4:00 a.m. in the morning and arriving at the factory by 5:00 a.m. Then he would work until 3:30 or later, go home, and go to bed early. "I wouldn't know what to do if I retired," he said in 1999. "It keeps me going." He continued to save, and toward the end of his life, when he was earning over $100,000 annually including overtime, he lived on only $600 a month while socking the rest into his investments or donating it.

Dawson became wealthy not because he was a financial wizard, but because he lived frugally, worked hard, and invested carefully. Keeping his eye on newspapers and television reports, he felt that anyone could do well enough in the stock market if they were careful. "I know what's good on the market and what's not good on the market," he said. "It's just as plain as day. I'm not going to jump into something that's not established, that doesn't have a reputation." The problem for most people, he noted, is that they are too lazy or greedy and want to make their fortunes quickly. "The trouble with a lot of people is they're looking for something for nothing—and it doesn't exist," he explained. "You have to get out there and work for it. I don't play no lotto, no numbers and all that stuff; that ain't my cup of tea."

Satisfaction for Dawson came through his work and through giving, which he learned was more rewarding than vacations and material possessions. As he once said, "I've owned big

Scholarship recipient Sonia Taggart once said she had assumed that the money came from "someone who would not miss the money he was giving away. Then I found out what he does, where he works, and I think that's what really floors you about him. He's so humble."

——— " ———

*"I've owned big homes
and big cars and that
don't excite me no more.
All that material stuff
doesn't excite me no
more. . . . I just want
people to say that I
helped somebody."*

——— " ———

homes and big cars and that don't excite me no more. All that material stuff doesn't excite me no more. . . . I just want people to say that I helped some-body." Looking back, he believed that his parents would have been proud of what he had done for others: "I'm on a mission fulfilling my parents' dreams. They wanted us to be something in life and stand for something."

Dawson died of a heart attack on November 2, 2002, in Highland Park, Michigan, at the age of 81. Two of his siblings, Luella Fuller and Clyde Dawson, survived him. He may have died in a humble one-bedroom apartment with few possessions to his name, but his legacy of giving and his belief in education lives on. In his will, he left his estate to the United Negro College Fund, which continues to use the money to help those in need achieve their dreams.

MAJOR INFLUENCES

Besides his parents, who taught him the values of saving and an educa-tion, Dawson greatly admired two American leaders: Franklin Delano Roosevelt and Reverend Martin Luther King, Jr. Roosevelt, he said, "gave the whole country a new start"; and King "gave black people hope when there wasn't none." King's example was particularly inspirational to him when it came to his spirit of giving. He once remarked, "Like Dr. King said, 'If I can help somebody, then my living will not be in vain' — that's how I want to be remembered."

MARRIAGE AND FAMILY

Dawson married Herneta Alberta Davis on February 21, 1942. The couple had a happy marriage for many years, but it ended in divorce in 1976. They had one daughter, JoAnn Dawson-Agee.

MEMORABLE EXPERIENCES

After word got out about Dawson's many charitable contributions, he was invited to appear on television shows and at public events. For example, in 1991 he was Grand Marshall at the city of Highland Park's Michigan Week parade. He appeared on the Oprah Winfrey show and other television programs, and during the Clinton administration, he was invited to the White House. Dawson enjoyed these events, which were his only indulgences in life besides the Burberry suits he liked to wear during church and college visits.

HONORS AND AWARDS

Michiganian of the Year: 1990
Outstanding Philanthropy Award (National Society of Fund Raising Executives): 1995
International Heritage Hall of Fame Honoree: 1996
Equal Opportunity Day Community Hero Award (National Urban League): 1996
Ossian Sweet Award: 1997, for donating to the United Negro College Fund
Living Legacy Award: 1997
Trumpet Award (Turner Broadcasting System): 1998

FURTHER READING

Books

Contemporary Black Biography, Vol. 39, 2003
Who's Who among African Americans, 2003

Periodicals

Black Enterprise, Mar. 2000, p.97; Feb. 2003, p.65
Detroit News, Nov. 7, 2002, p.2
Ebony, Oct. 1996, p.62
Jet, Jan. 31, 1994, p.23; Apr. 21, 1997, p.22; Dec. 29, 1997, p.61
Los Angeles Times, Nov. 8, 2002, p.B14

New York Times, Nov. 13, 2002, p.B10
People, June 7, 1999, p.103
Time, July 19, 1999, p.6

Online Articles

http://www.freep.com
   (*Detroit Free Press*, "An Unlikely Benefactor: A Forklift Operator's Frugal
   Life Lets Him Donate More than $1 Million toward Education," April
   25, 2001; "Matel Dawson Jr.: Forklift Operator Gave $1 Million," Nov. 5,
   2002)
http://www.media.wayne.edu/iws.back.issues/cn_11_14_02/Dawson.html
   (*Wayne State University*, "Wayne State Benefactor Matel Dawson Jr. Dies
   at 81," Nov. 14, 2002)

Online Databases

Biography Resource Center Online, 2003, articles from *Contemporary Black
Biography,* 2003, and *Who's Who among African Americans,* 2003

Lisa Leslie 1972-

American Professional Basketball Player with
the Los Angeles Sparks
Led the Sparks to Two Consecutive WNBA
Championships
Two-Time Winner of Olympic Gold Medals in
Women's Basketball

BIRTH

Lisa Deshaun Leslie was born on July 7, 1972, in Los Angeles,
California. Her father, Walter Leslie, left the family when she
was very young. She rarely saw him during her childhood, and

————  ————

*"We had no money and we
could have gone on welfare,
but my mom wanted to do
something she was proud of,"
Leslie recalled. "She sat us
down and said, 'This is what
I've got to do. I'm going to
buy a truck and learn how to
drive it. It's going to take time
for me to pay it off and get a
local route. I need you kids to
give me five years.'"*

———— **"** ————

he died when she was 12 years old. Her mother, Christine Leslie, was a postal worker who later bought an 18-wheeled truck and became a cross-country truck driver. She raised Lisa and her two sisters — Dionne, who is older, and Tiffany, who is younger — as a single mother. In 1995 Christine Leslie married Thomas Espinoza, a mechanic, and Lisa gained four younger stepbrothers.

YOUTH

Growing up, Leslie lived in several different parts of the Los Angeles area, including Carson, Compton, Gardena, and Inglewood. Money was always tight during her childhood, as her single mother struggled to make ends meet on her salary as a postal worker. Christine Leslie eventually decided to launch a new career as a truck driver. She sold the family home and used the money to buy an 18-wheeler. "We had no money and we could have gone on welfare, but my mom wanted to do something she was proud of," Lisa recalled. "She sat us down and said, 'This is what I've got to do. I'm going to buy a truck and learn how to drive it. It's going to take time for me to pay it off and get a local route. I need you kids to give me five years.'"

During the school year, Leslie and her sisters lived with relatives while their mother hauled goods back and forth across the country. Christine Leslie only managed to come home for a few days each month, and Lisa missed her terribly while she was away. "There were some sad times," she noted. "Mom had to travel so far and so long. But we understood she had to do it. It made me mature really fast. I had so much to do." In the summertime, Lisa and her sisters often accompanied their mother on the road, traveling to cities all around the country. They helped plot out routes on maps, showered at truck stops, and slept in the cab of their mother's rig. The sleeping compartment was only 36 inches wide, Lisa recalled. "All of us would jam in there. We had to hold on to each other. That helps us now. We all hold on to each other in a lot of ways."

Even as a little girl, Leslie was exceptionally tall. The daughter of parents who were both six feet, three inches tall, Lisa was taller than her second grade teacher. She stood six feet tall by the time she was 12 years old, and she reached her full adult height of six feet, five inches during high school. Other kids teased her about her height throughout her adolescence. "They called me Olive Oyl, they called me all sorts of things," she remembered. "The grown-ups mostly thought my height was beautiful, but the kids gave me a hard time." Fortunately, Leslie had a tall female role model in her very own home. "The closer I got to my mother's height, the more beautiful I felt," she noted. "She raised me to be confident and hold my head up."

Because of her height, people always assumed that Leslie played basketball. She actually resisted playing the sport for many years because so many people asked her about it. "I hated the association with basketball because I was so tall," she admitted. "I got so sick of everyone asking me. I developed this real bad attitude toward sports, especially basketball." Finally, a junior high classmate convinced her to try out for the school team. Leslie soon discovered that she could have an impact on the court without even trying. "We went 7-0," she remembered of her first season on the junior high team. "They'd throw me the ball, I'd catch it and make a layup. That's all I could do. I told the coach, 'If I fall down, I'm quitting.' And I didn't want to break a sweat. I hated to sweat. I was so prissy."

But Leslie became much more serious about basketball the following year. "I just changed my whole attitude," she admitted. "I guess it was my destiny but I never knew it." She credits an older cousin, Craig Simpson, with helping her improve her strength and conditioning. "Working with my cousin is how I got my skills. I told him I liked basketball, and that was it," she related. "My cousin made me do push-ups and sit-ups and then we'd work on my shots. I think it was at that point I learned how hard you had to work to get from one level to the next." Playing pick-up basketball games with Simpson and other boys also brought out Leslie's competitive instincts.

> *Leslie credits an older cousin, Craig Simpson, with helping her improve her strength and conditioning. "Working with my cousin is how I got my skills. I told him I liked basketball, and that was it," she related. "My cousin made me do push-ups and sit-ups and then we'd work on my shots. I think it was at that point I learned how hard you had to work to get from one level to the next."*

While still a student at Morningside High School, Leslie scored 101 points in the first half of a basketball game on February 8, 1990. The opposing team, South Torrance High, walked off at half time.

EDUCATION

By the time Leslie entered high school, her mother had secured a local truck route and settled the family in Inglewood. Leslie attended Morningside High School, where she earned a 3.5 grade-point average and was elected class president three times. She was also the starting center for the girls' varsity basketball team from the time she was a freshman. She led the Monarchs to a 125-9 record and two California state championships during her four-year high school career, averaging 26.9 points, 15 rebounds, and 6.9 blocked shots per game. She finished her career with 2,896 points (which ranked second in California girls' high school history) and set a new state record with 1,705 rebounds. She also played volleyball and competed in track, winning the state title in the high jump with a leap of 5 feet, 5 inches during her senior year.

During her junior year in 1989, Leslie became the first girl to dunk a basketball in a high school game (and only the second woman ever to dunk in competition). She learned that she could dunk by accident while she was fooling around with a tennis ball during track practice. "I started my attack, taking steps like boom, boom, boom. I was driving really hard with my knee in the air. And then I dunked it," she remembered of that day. "The track coach was like, 'What was that?' I dunked it so hard, with so much authority, he yelled for somebody to get a volleyball and told me to do the exact same thing and think about the high jump. I ran my approach and I dunked the volleyball. Then I got a basketball. I backed up again and dunked it. And I've been dunking ever since."

Leslie's dunk received notice in newspapers across the country. Yet she insisted that it was not a big deal to her. "Dunking is something that guys care more about than girls," she noted. "There's something about jumping that seems to fascinate guys. Girls are more like, as long as the ball goes in, who cares how you got it there?" During her senior year, however, Leslie enjoyed entertaining her fellow students by performing dunks during school pep rallies.

Perhaps the most notable feat of Leslie's high school basketball career came during her senior year. The Morningside girls' basketball team had a longstanding tradition of helping a senior captain to score as many points as possible during her last regular-season home game. In Leslie's last home game of 1990, she took full advantage of this tradition. As the game unfolded against a completely overmatched team from South Torrance High School, Leslie's teammates fed her the ball repeatedly. Leslie scored 49 points in the first quarter and 52 in the second for a total of 101 at halftime. She

"Dunking is something that guys care more about than girls," Leslie noted. "There's something about jumping that seems to fascinate guys. Girls are more like, as long as the ball goes in, who cares how you got it there?"

seemed certain to break the all-time single-game national high-school scoring record of 105 points set by former star and current NBA commentator Cheryl Miller. But several South Torrance players had fouled out or been injured during the first half, and the opposing coach refused to play the second half. He decided to forfeit the game rather than force his team to endure further embarrassment. Leslie was disappointed that she was denied an opportunity to see how many points she could have scored. "Anyone that can count knows that I would have had [the record]," she said afterward. "They just shortened the game. I feel that I have the record."

Leslie's 100-point game received coverage in the national news as well as *Sports Illustrated.* She went on to be named Naismith National Prep Player of the Year for 1990. By the time she graduated from high school later that year, she was widely considered to be the best girls' high school player in the country. She was heavily recruited by every major college basketball program, but she ultimately decided to remain close to home and attend the University of Southern California (USC) so her mother could watch her play. Leslie balanced her school work with her time playing basketball with the USC Trojans, graduating from USC in 1994 with a bachelor's degree in communications. She returned to school in 2002 to begin working toward a master's degree in business administration.

CAREER HIGHLIGHTS

College — USC Trojans

Leslie's basketball career really began while she was in college. When she entered USC in the fall of 1990, the women's basketball team was in a rebuilding phase. The Trojans had posted a disappointing 8-19 record the previous year, but they had recruited several promising young players in addition to Leslie. Leslie turned in an outstanding freshman season, averaging 19.4 points and 10.0 rebounds per game to lead all freshmen in the nation in both categories. She also became the first freshman ever named to the All-Pacific 10 (Pac 10) Conference Team. But Leslie did encounter some problems defending against stronger, more experienced players. In fact, she set a school record for most personal fouls in a season. "I think it was a revelation to Lisa that there were weaknesses in her game that other people could exploit," said USC Coach Marianne Stanley. Although the Trojans received an invitation to the National Collegiate Athletic Association (NCAA) tournament, they lost in the early rounds.

Leslie continued her strong performance as a sophomore, averaging 20.4 points and 8.4 rebounds per game. She was named All-Pac 10 for the second time and also received first-team All-American honors. USC advanced to the regional finals of the 1991-92 NCAA tournament before being eliminated. As a junior Leslie averaged 18.7 points and 9.8 rebounds per game, which helped her earn all-conference and All-American honors once again. USC made the NCAA tournament for the third straight year, only to fall once again in an early-round contest.

Leslie averaged a career-best 21.9 points and 12.3 rebounds per game during her senior season in 1993-94. USC posted a 26-4 record and advanced to the regional finals of the NCAA tournament, where they were knocked out by Louisiana Tech. Still, Leslie's strong performance garnered a number of prestigious awards. She was named all-conference for the fourth straight year and earned All-American honors for the third consecutive season. She also received the NCAA National Player of the Year and Naismith College Player of the Year awards for 1994.

Leslie drives to the basket while playing for the USC Trojans against the UCLA Bruins, 1993.

By the end of her four years at USC, Leslie's career totals of 2,414 points, 1,214 rebounds, and 321 blocks all ranked as new Pac 10 records. Leslie took enormous pride in her college accomplishments, and she enjoyed her reputation as one of the country's best female players. When she graduated in 1994, though, no professional women's basketball league existed in the United States. As a result, she set her sights on representing her country in international competition. "A lot of coaches have said I have the potential to be the kind of player who can help women's basketball reach more people," she stated. "I think we do need that one star that even people who aren't familiar with the game can recognize. It not only gets the attention of the public, it gets the attention of the kids who will grow up to be the next superstars."

> "A lot of coaches have said I have the potential to be the kind of player who can help women's basketball reach more people," Leslie said. "I think we do need that one star that even people who aren't familiar with the game can recognize. It not only gets the attention of the public, it gets the attention of the kids who will grow up to be the next superstars."

U.S. National Women's Basketball Team

By the time Leslie graduated from USC in 1994, she had already gained a great deal of experience in international competition. As a junior in high school, for example, she represented the United States at the 1989 Junior World Championships. Two years later, as a freshman in college, she helped the U.S. team clinch a gold medal at the World University Games. Leslie was the youngest player invited to try out for the U.S. Olympic Team in 1992. As the last player cut from the roster before the Games, she narrowly missed achieving her dream of playing in the Olympics. Later that year she became a member of the World Championship qualifying team. Her performance in that competition earned her the honor of being named USA Basketball Female Player of the Year for 1993.

Leslie also helped the U.S. National Women's Basketball Team earn a gold medal at the 1994 Goodwill Games. She was virtually unstoppable in the tournament, making an amazing 72 percent of her shots from the field. Later that year, Leslie and her American teammates competed for the World Championship in Spain. They were deeply disappointed when they lost in the semifinals of the tournament and had to settle for a bronze medal. "That left a bad taste in our mouths," Leslie recalled.

In the fall of 1994, Leslie signed a contract to play professional basketball for the Sicilgesso team in Alcamo, Italy. She became a star of the European basketball league, averaging 22.6 points and 11.7 rebounds per game. She also grew more aggressive and confident with each passing week. "I just got stronger, and that changed my game mentally more than anything," she explained. "For the first time, I could move big people around. All my life I'd heard people talking about my 'potential' in basketball. In Italy, for the first time, I understood what all that meant. When I got stronger, I could play very well against bigger, older, and more experienced players." Still, Leslie did not enjoy the experience of playing in Italy. "It's hell being overseas," she admitted. "It's lonely." As a result, she ended her contract with Sicilgesso after one season and returned to the United States.

In 1995 Leslie competed for a roster spot on the U.S. Olympic Team that would compete in the 1996 Summer Olympic Games in Atlanta, Georgia. She was one of 12 players selected from among the top 60 female basketball players in the country. The impressive roster included legends like Katrina McClain and Teresa Edwards, as well as young NCAA stars such as Rebecca Lobo, Sheryl Swoopes, and Dawn Staley. "Atlanta will be an opportunity for us to go down in history as one of the greatest teams ever," Leslie declared. "It'll be a showcase for us as role models—not only for girls who play basketball but for women in general."

In preparation for the 1996 Olympics, the U.S. National Women's Basketball Team played an intense and grueling schedule. Over the course of a year, they traveled over 100,000 miles and played 52 games on four continents. The American women went undefeated in their Olympic warmup games. Leslie contributed 17.4 points and 7.0 rebounds per game to lead the team in both categories.

The U.S. team continued its dominance during the Olympic tournament, winning six straight games to reach the gold-medal match. Leslie led the team with 19.5 points and 7.3 rebounds per game, and she set a new Olympic single-game record by scoring 35 points against Japan. Leslie also showed her mettle in the gold medal match against a tough Brazil team. She played poorly in the first half of the game, but she came back strong in the second half to score 29 points on 12 of 14 shooting. The U.S. team won the game 111-87 and claimed the Olympic gold medal. Afterward, some observers claimed that the American team was the best in the history of women's basketball. Best of all, their success generated a great deal of interest in the sport. "We accomplished what we set out to do," Leslie stated.

Leslie leaps to the basket while playing for the U.S. national team in the 1996 Olympics.

"We tried to get women's basketball to the next level. Our game speaks for itself, but now our names are in the public eye and that's the thing that took the NBA from one level to the next."

WNBA — Los Angeles Sparks

After achieving her dream of winning an Olympic gold medal, Leslie thought about taking a break from basketball. "I played 10 years straight to be an Olympian," she explained. "I'm tired." She decided to pursue a career as a fashion model, even going so far as to sign a contract with the prestigious Wilhelmina modeling agency. But Leslie was lured back to basketball a short time later by the formation of two women's professional basketball leagues in the United States. The first of these leagues was the American Basketball League (ABL), which formed in 1996. Due to poor planning and recruiting, however, it failed after three seasons. The second and more successful league, the Women's National Basketball Association (WNBA), was formed in 1997.

The WNBA enjoyed financial support from the NBA, the popular men's professional league. The league also attracted more fans by scheduling its games during the summer, when NBA and college basketball teams did not play. The WNBA started out with eight teams based in major cities

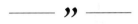

"We accomplished what we set out to do," Leslie said about winning the gold medal at the 1996 Olympics. "We tried to get women's basketball to the next level. Our game speaks for itself, but now our names are in the public eye and that's the thing that took the NBA from one level to the next."

across the United States. Most of these teams built their rosters around key players from the gold-medal winning U.S. Women's Olympic Basketball Team, like Leslie, Rebecca Lobo, and Sheryl Swoopes. Leslie, for example, signed a contract to play for the Los Angeles Sparks, based in her hometown. "I'm excited to have the opportunity to continue my basketball career in the United States, especially in Los Angeles," she stated.

The WNBA completed its first season in the summer of 1997. Leslie immediately established herself as one of the league's premier players. She led the league in rebounding (with an average of 9.5 per game), ranked second in blocked shots (2.1 per game), and finished third in scoring (15.9 points per game). In recognition of her performance, she was named to the All-WNBA first team at the conclusion of the season. Despite Leslie's heroics, however, the Sparks posted only a 14-14 record and they failed to make the playoffs.

In 1998 the WNBA expanded to include two more teams and extended the season to 30 games. The Sparks finished with a disappointing 12-18 record, but Leslie once again ranked among the league leaders in several statistical categories. She led the WNBA in rebounds with 10.2, ranked second in blocks with 2.1, and finished third in scoring with 19.6. Due to her team's poor performance, however, she was only selected to the All-WNBA second team.

——— " ———

Leslie was devastated by the loss when her team was swept in the 2000 conference finals. "She came home, went to her room, and cried her heart out," her mother recalled. "We were going to have lots of friends and family over for dinner because we all wanted to tell Lisa how well she had done and how proud we were of her. But Lisa said, 'Mom, I need to be alone right now. It hurts too much.'"

——— 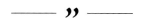 ———

The WNBA added two more teams and expanded to a 32-game schedule for the 1999 season. The league also held its first All-Star Game that year. Leslie played center for the Western Conference and was named most valuable player of the game. "I felt really honored to have this award," she stated. "I thought the crowd was great. They got me totally fired up and the atmosphere was awesome."

The Sparks played inconsistently for much of the 1999 season but finished strong for a 20-12 record. Although Leslie's personal statistics declined to 15.6 points, 7.8 rebounds, and 1.5 blocks per game, she was pleased about her team's improved performance. The Sparks won their first playoff series and advanced to the conference championship, where they faced the two-time defending WNBA champion Houston Comets. Leslie and her teammates played well but lost the series, two games to one. "I think this Comets team knows that they just went through the best team in the WNBA and I wish them the best of luck," Leslie said afterward. Houston went on to win its third consecutive WNBA title.

As the 2000 WNBA season began, Leslie vowed to bring home a championship ring. She contributed 17.8 points, 9.6 rebounds, and 2.3 blocks per game to help her team post the best record in the league at 28-4. The

Leslie grabs a rebound during a 1997 WNBA game.

Sparks' amazing regular season performance gave them home-court advantage in the playoffs, but they were not able to capitalize on it. The promising season ended in heartbreaking fashion when Los Angeles was swept in the conference finals by Houston. Leslie was devastated by the loss. "She came home, went to her room, and cried her heart out," her mother recalled. "We were going to have lots of friends and family over for dinner because we all wanted to tell Lisa how well she had done and how proud we were of her. But Lisa said, 'Mom, I need to be alone right now. It hurts too much.'"

Winning Two WNBA Championships

Leslie did not wallow in her disappointment over the Sparks' 2000 season. Instead, she decided to do her part to help prepare the team for the 2001 campaign. She hired a personal trainer and began working out twice a day. She also performed drills with the Sparks' new head coach, former Los Angeles Lakers star Michael Cooper. "I watched tapes of last year's conference finals and decided I had to become more aggressive and more mentally tough," she explained. "I also wanted to improve my passing, my shooting percentage, and my ability to drive and dribble, left and right. I wanted to solidify my post game, too. It was time to make an investment in myself."

A smiling Leslie shows off her trophy after the Sparks won the 2001 WNBA championship.

Leslie's hard work paid off during the 2001 WNBA season. Many observers claimed that she transformed herself into the most dominant player in the league. Leslie averaged 19.5 points, 9.6 rebounds, and 2.29 blocked shots per game to lead the Sparks to an amazing 34-5 record. "I call her The Package now," said Sparks assistant coach Glenn McDonald. "She can shoot the jumper, she can run the lane, she can shoot the hook, she can shoot the three [point shot]. She does everything." Opposing coaches, meanwhile, admitted that defending against Leslie was a big challenge. "In the past, physical play may have distracted her or officiating might take her out of her game," said Charlotte Sting Coach Anne Donovan. "But this year she was very focused, never distracted, always confident and poised and always showed great leadership with the Sparks. Her game was at her peak."

The Sparks advanced through the playoffs to the WNBA Finals, where they defeated the Charlotte Sting in a two-game sweep. Leslie scored 24 points, grabbed 13 rebounds, blocked 7 shots, and added 6 assists in the final game. She was named Most Valuable Player of the regular season, the All-Star Game, and the championship series—thus becoming the first WNBA player to win all three awards in a single season. Afterward, Cooper called it "one of the best [seasons] I've ever seen by a professional athlete playing basketball. From training camp to the final day, she got on a roll and then went to another level whenever we needed to win. And not only did she go up, she made everybody on the team go up." For her part, Leslie was thrilled with the results of the season. "I'm not sure I'd call this championship getting the monkey off my back," she stated. "What I did was find the heart I needed to win the big games, and that feels great."

As the 2002 season got underway for the reigning WNBA champs, opposing teams focused solely on stopping Leslie. She faced double- and triple-team defenses all year, which caused her statistics to decline to 16.9 points, 10.4 rebounds, and 2.9 blocks per game. But she still managed to accomplish some impressive feats. On July 30, 2002, Leslie became the first woman ever to dunk a basketball during a professional game. A short time later, Leslie became the WNBA's all-time leading scorer as well as the first player in the league to score 3,000 points in her career. Even more satisfying for Leslie, the Sparks earned the best record in the western conference and defeated the New York Liberty to claim their second consecutive WNBA title. Once again, Leslie was named Most Valuable Player of the championship series.

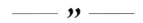

The Sparks started off strong in 2003, posting a 15-3 record during the first half of the season. But Leslie injured her knee in the All-Star Game and was forced to sit out the next 11 games. The Sparks struggled without their star center, posting a 4-7 record and dropping out of first place in the Western Conference. After Leslie returned to the lineup, however, the Sparks won their remaining five games to finish with a 24-10 record for the year. Leslie, meanwhile, finished the season with her usual dazzling numbers, contributing 18.4 points, 10.0 rebounds, and 2.74 blocks per game. After defeating the Sacramento Monarchs in the conference finals, the Sparks seemed poised to win their third straight WNBA crown.

Leslie was thrilled with the results of the 2001 season. "I'm not sure I'd call this championship getting the monkey off my back. What I did was find the heart I needed to win the big games, and that feels great."

The Sparks' opponent in the WNBA finals was the Detroit Shock, a young team that had earned the best overall record in the league in 2003 after posting the worst overall record the previous year. Leslie and her teammates used their playoff experience to trounce the Shock in the first game in Los Angeles. Leslie contributed 23 points, 12 rebounds, and 3 blocks in that contest. But the series moved to Detroit for the two remaining games. The Sparks suffered a heartbreaking one-point overtime loss in game 2. This set the stage for the deciding game 3, which was played before a WNBA-record crowd of 22,076 people. The Shock controlled Leslie with stifling defense, and she fouled out in the final minutes after scoring only 13 points. The Shock won the game and the WNBA title, denying Leslie and the Sparks a three-peat. "I would have to say this is probably the most physical game I've ever played in my life, these last two games," Leslie said afterward. "I guess I have the bruises on my face to show it."

Two New York Liberty players can't stop Leslie during this 2003 game in Madison Square Garden.

Making an Impact on the Game

Over her six-year WNBA career, Leslie has averaged 17.6 points, 9.5 rebounds, and 2.27 blocked shots per game. Her fluid play has earned her the nickname "Smooth," and her competitive nature and well-rounded game have won over legions of fans. In fact, her number 9 Sparks jersey is the top seller in the WNBA. Of course, as one of the superstars of the league, Leslie is often the focus of boos from fans of opposing teams.

Throughout her outstanding WNBA career, Leslie has also continued to represent the United States in international women's basketball. In 1998 she led the American team to a gold medal in the World Championships. Her contributions of 17.1 points and 8.8 rebounds per game earned her USA Basketball Female Athlete of the Year honors for 1998. In 2000 Leslie won a second gold medal at the Olympic Games in Sydney, Australia. She averaged 15.8 points and 7.9 rebounds per game during the Olympic tournament. In 2002 Leslie helped the American team repeat its gold-medal performance at the World Championships. She was named Most Valuable Player of the tournament in recognition of her stellar play.

All of these accomplishments have elevated Leslie to the pinnacle of her sport and made her a role model for countless young women. By combining toughness and skill with femininity and flair, Leslie has helped increase the visibility and popularity of women's basketball. "When I'm playing, I'll sweat and talk trash. However, off the court I'm lipstick, heels, and short skirts. I'm very feminine, mild-mannered, and sensitive," she explained. "I'd definitely like some little girl to be looking at me as someone who's a woman, intelligent, attractive, and an athlete."

As much as she has done for her sport, Leslie expresses appreciation for the opportunities basketball has given her. "I always wonder what would have happened to me if I hadn't picked up that ball [in junior high]," she noted. "I might be working at a McDonald's. I might be at a local junior college. I don't know. Basketball's done a lot for me. Put me through college and let me go around the world."

Leslie hopes to take advantage of her time in the spotlight to influence the lives of young people. "Everything in my life is a blessing," she stated. "Right now I'm in that window of opportunity. I might be hot, people know my name. But that window

By combining toughness and skill with femininity and flair, Leslie has helped increase the visibility and popularity of women's basketball. "When I'm playing, I'll sweat and talk trash. However, off the court I'm lipstick, heels, and short skirts. I'm very feminine, mild-mannered, and sensitive," she explained. "I'd definitely like some little girl to be looking at me as someone who's a woman, intelligent, attractive, and an athlete."

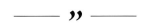

only stays open for a short period of time. When it closes, it will be someone else's turn. I understand that while the window is open, I give all I can. I do the autographs, smile at people, try to touch lives in the ways I can. There are many things I like to do in life, but I recognize that while the attention is on me, people are listening. So I have to use my ability to hopefully help some kids want to set goals and do something with their lives."

Leslie plans to continue her WNBA career for several more years. She has also been selected for the U.S. Olympic Women's Basketball Team that will compete in 2004 in Athens, Greece, and she hopes to add a third gold medal to her trophy case at that time. "Overall, in regards to my career, I have fulfilled a lot of the goals I have set," she noted. "But even when I found myself the best at certain levels—whether high school, college, or the pros —there is always something I could learn and do better. That's my attitude. The day I stop doing that is the day I'm going to be done."

"Overall, in regards to my career, I have fulfilled a lot of the goals I have set," Leslie noted. "But even when I found myself the best at certain levels — whether high school, college, or the pros — there is always something I could learn and do better. That's my attitude. The day I stop doing that is the day I'm going to be done."

HOME AND FAMILY

Leslie, who is single, earns well over $1 million per year from her WNBA salary and endorsements. She lives in a large, split-level home in Los Angeles with a view of the ocean. She shares her home with a pit bull puppy named Lennox. Leslie remains very close to her mother, who lives nearby in a home that was a gift from her daughter.

HOBBIES AND OTHER INTERESTS

Leslie enjoys playing cards and board games in her spare time. Since 1996, when she signed a contract with the prestigious Wilhelmina agency, she has also enjoyed a second career as a fashion model. She has appeared in a number of national magazines and has walked the runway at several fashion shows. "I love all types of modeling, whether it be on a runway in front of hundreds of people, or the photo shoot where it's just me and the photographer," she explained. "It gives me a chance to let people know that there's much more to Lisa Leslie. I also like to show girls that you can be tough and feminine, too."

Leslie hopes to become a sportscaster when her basketball career is over. To that end, she has provided color commentary for USC basketball games and worked as a correspondent for "NBA Inside Stuff." She has also tried her hand at acting, appearing as a guest star on such TV shows as "Moesha," "Hang Time," "Sister Sister," and "Who Wants to Be a Millionaire?"

Leslie enjoys the moment, after winning a gold medal with Team USA in the 2000 Olympics.

Leslie is very active in charity work, particularly for causes that serve children. She works with several programs designed to raise the self-esteem of young girls, and she personally sponsors six foster children. She is also a national spokesperson for the Big Brothers/Big Sisters organization. "I think it's very important that kids have role models to look up to," she noted. "My mom made sure that I was raised properly and was given all the support I needed. Big Brothers/Big Sisters of America is focused on providing youth with the necessary support when they can't receive it at home." Leslie is a board member of her church, and she also has donated money to help her former high school improve its athletic facilities.

HONORS AND AWARDS

High School All-American: 1989, 1990
Naismith Prep Player of the Year: 1990
Pacific 10 Conference Freshman of the Year: 1990-91
NCAA Women's Basketball Freshman of the Year: 1990-91
All-Pacific 10 Conference: 1990-91, 1991-92, 1992-93, 1993-94
NCAA All-American: 1991-92, 1992-93, 1993-94
NCAA National Player of the Year: 1993-94
Naismith College Player of the Year: 1993-94
USA Basketball Female Athlete of the Year: 1993, 1998, 2000
Women's Basketball World Championship: 1994, bronze medal; 1998, gold
    medal; 2002, gold medal
Olympic Women's Basketball: 1996, gold medal; 2000, gold medal
All-WNBA: 1997, 2000, 2001, 2002, 2003
WNBA All-Star: 1999-2003
WNBA All-Star Game Most Valuable Player: 1999, 2001, 2002
WNBA Most Valuable Player: 2001
WNBA Championship Most Valuable Player: 2001
WNBA Championship: 2001, 2002 (with Los Angeles Sparks)
Team Sportswoman of the Year (Women's Sports Foundation): 2001
ESPY Award as Best WNBA Player: 2002
Women's Basketball World Championship Most Valuable Player: 2002
Most Outstanding High School Girls Basketball Player of the Past 20 Years
    (*USA Today*): 2002

FURTHER READING

Books

Corbett, Sara. *Venus to the Hoop: A Gold Medal Year in Women's Basketball,*
    1997
Kelley, Brent. *Lisa Leslie,* 2001 (juvenile)
Ponti, James. *WNBA: Stars of Women's Basketball,* 1998
Stewart, Mark. *Lisa Leslie: Queen of the Court,* 1998
VanDerveer, Tara. *Shooting from the Outside: How a Coach and Her Olympic
    Team Transformed Women's Basketball,* 1998
Who's Who in the World, 2003

Periodicals

Cleveland Plain Dealer, Aug. 4, 1996, p.D11; Feb. 7, 1997, p.D5
Current Biography Yearbook, 1998

Detroit News, Sep. 17, 2003, p.E6

Los Angeles Times, Jan. 12, 1989, Sports sec., p.12; June 21, 1997, Sports sec., p.3; Aug. 8, 1999, Magazine sec., p.10; Aug. 25, 2001, p.D1; May 14, 2002, p.D1; Aug. 1, 2002, p.D1; Sep. 17, 2003, Sports sec., p.1

Ms., Dec. 2002/Jan. 2003, p.49

New York Times, Dec. 5, 1993, sec. 8, p.8; July 11, 2003, p.D5

People, Aug. 19, 1996, p.42; June 30, 1997, p.109

Sport, July 1997, p.46

Sports Illustrated, Feb. 19, 1990, p.30; Dec. 3, 1990, p.92; Nov. 25, 1991, p.78; Sep. 10, 2001, p.46; Sep. 1, 2003, p.6

Sports Illustrated Women, May/June 2002, p.86

Vogue, May 1996, p.288

Women's Sports and Fitness, Nov./Dec. 1996, p.50

USA Today, May 1, 2002, p.C7

Online Articles

http://www.usolympicteam.com/10_questions/071702basketball.html
   (*USA 2002*, "Ten Questions for Basketball's Lisa Leslie," July 17, 2002)
http://www.detnews.com
   (*Detroit News*, "Shock Defense Stymies Leslie," Sep. 17, 2003)

Online Databases

Biography Resource Center Online, 2003, article from *Notable Sports Figures,* 2003

ADDRESS

Lisa Leslie
Los Angeles Sparks
555 North Nash Street
El Segundo, CA 90245

WORLD WIDE WEB SITES

http://www.wnba.com
http://www.usabasketball.com
http://www.usolympicteam.com

LINKIN PARK

Chester Bennington 1976-
Rob Bourdon 1979-
Brad Delson 1977-
Dave Farrell (Phoenix) 1977-
Joe Hahn 1977-
Mike Shinoda 1977-

American Rap-Rock Band

EARLY YEARS

The rap-rock group known as Linkin Park includes six members: Chester Bennington (singer); Rob Bourdon (drums);

Brad Delson (guitar); Dave Farrell, who is known as Phoenix (bass); Joe Hahn (DJ); and Mike Shinoda (rapper).

The connections among the group's members reach all the way back to their student days. Delson and Shinoda have known each other since junior high school, while Shinoda met Hahn at the Art Center College of Design in Pasadena. Phoenix was Delson's roommate in college, and Bourdon, who also attended the Art Center College of Design, first met Delson when he was in high school. At least part of the band's success can be attributed to how well and how long most of them have known each other, and to the goals and values they share.

Brad Delson

Brad Delson was born in Los Angeles on December 1, 1977. He began studying the guitar in elementary school, and in seventh grade he met Mike Shinoda. After graduating from Agoura High School, where he met future band member Rob Bourdon, he went to the University of California at Los Angeles (UCLA), where he majored in communications. He divided his time at college between studying, writing songs with Shinoda, and serving as an intern at Zomba Music, where he learned all about what it takes for an artist or a band to get a recording contract. This experience would prove valuable later on, when Delson and his own band were trying to attract the attention of a major recording label.

Delson seriously considered applying to law school, but by the time he graduated from UCLA he had already gotten together with his roommate, Dave Farrell (Phoenix), and his childhood friend Mike Shinoda to form a group called Xero. Rather than pursuing a career as a lawyer, he decided to stick with the band and see what happened. "I'm glad I took the risk," he says.

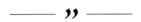

Delson seriously considered applying to law school, but by the time he graduated from UCLA he had already gotten together with his roommate, Dave Farrell (Phoenix), and his childhood friend Mike Shinoda to form a group called Xero (pronounced "Zero"). Rather than pursuing a career as a lawyer, he decided to stick with the band and see what happened. "I'm glad I took the risk," he says, although it wasn't easy for him to be unemployed while his friends moved on to careers or graduate school.

——— " ———

In 1991 Shinoda attended a rock concert featuring the metal band Anthrax and the rap group Public Enemy. "It was the first concert I'd ever been to, and it was this mixing of all these different types of music," he explains. "They played 'Bring the Noise' at the end of the show, and that left a mark on me. I always wanted to do something that mixed these styles of music."

——— " ———

Mike Shinoda

Michael Kenji Shinoda was born in Los Angeles on February 11, 1977, a second-generation Japanese-American whose father had spent time in a U.S. internment camp during World War II. At that time, the United States was at war with Japan. Some Americans worried that Japanese and Japanese-American people living and working in the U.S. might be traitors who would sabotage the American war effort — even though most of them, like Mike's father, thought of themselves as loyal Americans. In 1942 President Franklin Delano Roosevelt ordered that people of Japanese descent should be evacuated from the West Coast, and about 120,000 people were confined to these camps until the war was over. About two-thirds of them were native-born American citizens. They were forced to sell their homes and were sent to live in camps surrounded by barbed wire.

Born years later, Mike Shinoda avoided these hardships. He developed an early interest in music after he started taking piano lessons when he was six. "At first I went because my mom told me to — I wasn't all that excited about it," he says. "Eventually, though, I got really into it." He played mostly classical music until he was 13. Then he told his piano teacher that what he really wanted to play was jazz, blues, and even hip-hop. Because she didn't have any training in this kind of music, she suggested he buy a keyboard and try to teach himself. "I got a sampler," he recalls, "started making beats and playing around with . . . digital-based music."

As a junior high school student, Shinoda was interested in art, computers, and hip-hop. He would practice rapping by listening to Run DMC, LL Cool J, Grandmaster Flash, and others. Soon he was making up his own raps and performing them for his friends at school. Then in 1991 Shinoda attended a rock concert featuring the metal band Anthrax and the rap group Public Enemy. "It was the first concert I'd ever been to, and it was this mixing of all these different types of music," he explains. "They played

'Bring the Noise' at the end of the show, and that left a mark on me. I always wanted to do something that mixed these styles of music." Soon afterward, he got together with his childhood friend Brad Delson and began writing songs.

After graduating from Agoura High School with Delson, Shinoda majored in illustration at the Art Center College of Design in Pasadena, where he met Joe Hahn and Rob Bourdon. They joined with Shinoda and Delson to form Xero. Mike remembers how exhausting it was to balance his schedule as an art school student with his budding career as a musician: "I'd do classes from nine to four, four to seven, and seven to ten at night. I'd go from there to band practice in Hollywood for two or three hours, then all the way back to my parents' house and work on paintings until I couldn't do it anymore. Then I'd get up in the morning and do it all again." But his hard work paid off, and he graduated from college.

Phoenix

Phoenix was born David Farrell in Massachusetts on February 8, 1977. He studied classical violin for nine years and also played the cello when he was growing up. "There's a huge advantage to having played an instrument when I was younger," he admits, "not only in terms of dexterity, but in having a basis in music theory and developing an ear for music. You can learn a ton about composition and structure from Mozart."

After graduating from high school he went to UCLA, where he was Brad Delson's roommate and majored in philosophy. By the time he earned his bachelor of arts degree (B.A.) in 1999, he was being called "Phoenix," a nickname that started as a joke after he and some friends watched the Ben Stiller film *Mystery Men*.

By that point Delson and Shinoda had formed the band. But they didn't have a bass player, so they asked Phoenix to join them.

Rob Bourdon

Robert Bourdon was born in Los Angeles on January 20, 1979. Even as

"There's a huge advantage to having played an instrument when I was younger," Phoenix admits, "not only in terms of dexterity, but in having a basis in music theory and developing an ear for music. You can learn a ton about composition and structure from Mozart."

a toddler, he showed a passion for concentration and hard work: he once spent three hours learning to tie his own shoes. In third grade his parents took him to an Aerosmith concert—his mother was a former girlfriend of the band's drummer, Joey Kramer. The experience inspired him to start playing the drums himself.

Bourdon met Brad Delson at Agoura High School, and soon after that he started jamming with Brad and Mike. After graduation he worked as a waiter and in a bowling alley and even studied accounting at Santa Monica College. He ended up at the Art Center College of Design, where Mike Shinoda was a fellow illustration major. But Bourdon left after a year to try to make a living as a freelance illustrator. Among other things, he designed monsters and robots for the film industry. But he continued to jam with his high school friends whenever he could find the time.

Joe Hahn

Joseph Hahn was born in Los Angeles on March 15, 1977. His main interest when he was growing up was not so much music but the "sonic collages" that could be created by mixing sounds from different recordings, scratching records (see box on page 82), and adding keyboard loops and other bits of sound.

Hahn attended Art Center College of Design, where he met Mike Shinoda. But Hahn left college after his first year. He had already joined Xero as a DJ at this point, although he thought of it as a hobby rather than a possible career. The band now had five members—Delson, Shinoda, Phoenix, Bourdon, and Hahn—as well as a lead vocalist, Mark Wakefield.

Chester Bennington

Chester Bennington was born on March 20, 1976, in Phoenix, Arizona. His parents split up when he was 11 and he stayed with his father, who was a police officer. Bennington began singing before he was in kindergarten, but after that his musical tastes changed rapidly. "When I was in middle school, I was very into hip-hop," he recalls. "But when I went into high school I discovered punk rock, and that really changed my world."

"When I was in middle school, I was very into hip-hop," Bennington recalls. "But when I went into high school I discovered punk rock, and that really changed my world."

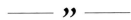

Bennington had a difficult childhood and adolescence. As a child, he suffered five years of sexual abuse. As a young teen, he became addicted to alcohol and drugs, including cocaine and methamphetamines. He dropped out of high school and worked at a number of minimum wage jobs. He was homeless for a period of time.

Soon he began turning his difficult experiences into music by writing songs for a hard rock band in Arizona called Grey Daze. He stayed with Grey Daze through most of the 1990s, but finally realized that he was not getting anywhere as an artist. "It was time for me to move on," he says.

FORMING LINKIN PARK

By 1995 Xero consisted of Delson, Shinoda, Bourdon, Phoenix, Hahn, and Mark Wakefield. But Wakefield never really fit in comfortably with the rest of the group, and by 1998 it became clear to the group that they would

What Is New Metal?

It's been called by many names, including rap-rock and rap-metal, but "new metal" music (also spelled "nu metal") commonly refers to a style that appeared in the late 1980s and early 1990s. New metal bands combine rap, metal, and punk styles, which is why they are also associated with the term "fusion." Many of their songs express anger, depression, and even violence, with the vocalists shouting, singing, and rapping. The lyrics are deeply personal and reflect the emotional turmoil of adolescence.

Distorted guitars and hip-hop rhythms are typical of new metal, as is an onstage DJ who "scratches" records and plays "samples." Scratching is when DJs stop the records from spinning with their hands and then move them back and forth to produce a rhythmic scratching sound. Samples are brief passages of music or sound from existing recordings that are reproduced digitally and then reused in a new song. Limp Bizkit, which uses a full-time DJ with lyrics delivered in rap style and often shouted or screamed, is consider a typical new metal band.

have to find a new vocalist. A mutual friend contacted Bennington in Phoenix and sent him Xero's demo tape. Bennington, who had always wanted to be a rock star, flew out to Los Angeles to audition two days later. When he heard the band play, he thought to himself, "This is the one. This [is] the golden ticket to get inside Willy Wonka's chocolate factory." He left his Phoenix-based band and quit his day-job at a digital services firm to join Xero.

What's in a Name?

One of the first things the band did when they started getting serious about their music in 1996 was to call themselves Hybrid Theory, a name that reflected their interest in combining existing musical styles. They began fusing hip-hop, rock, and electronic music in a way that had never been heard before. But before they could make a name for themselves, Limp Bizkit, Korn, and other "fusion" groups released albums that did the same thing. Rather than becoming discouraged, Hybrid Theory decided to continue doing what they were doing, but to do it better and differently than anyone else.

The group played showcases for more than 40 different record labels, but everyone turned them down. Then, after one of their first live performances at the Hollywood club known as Whiskey, they were offered a publishing (songwriting) contract by Zomba Music, where Brad had been an intern. This was great for their self-confidence, but it still wasn't a recording contract of their own. They continued to work hard on developing their own unique sound and started promoting their music over the Internet. They began visiting online chat rooms, uploading MP3s of their songs, and sending out free tapes and T-shirts via their web site. "We used the Internet as a tool to find people who were interested in the style of music we were playing, and to see if they wanted to help us by getting the word out," Phoenix explains. Group members would even pretend to be fans themselves, urging others to "check out this new band."

"The first album [Hybrid Theory] *has feelings of confusion and anger and paranoia,"Shinoda explains. "We were writing about those from the perspective of young 20-year-old guys."*

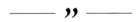

Finally, in 1999, they were offered a contract by Warner Brothers Records. There was only one problem: Warner Brothers had already signed another group called Hybrid, so they had to change their name again. This time they settled on Lincoln Park, the name of a park in Santa Monica near their rehearsal studio. But when they tried to register a domain name on the Internet, they discovered that the name "lincolnpark.com" was already taken, so they changed the spelling to "Linkin." This name seemed to reflect not only their own unique approach to making music but their effort to reach out to fans everywhere, since so many towns in America have their own "Lincoln Park."

CAREER HIGHLIGHTS

Hybrid Theory

It took Linkin Park more than two years to write all the songs for their first album, *Hybrid Theory*. But their web-savvy approach to marketing their music paid off. When the album was released in October 2000, it climbed rapidly to the Top Ten on the *Billboard* Top 200 chart and stayed there. By March 2001 it had gone platinum.

The songs on the album are mostly about difficult relationships. They combine punk and rap-metal styles, with the influence of hip-hop particularly strong in the lyrics and rhythms. Shinoda and Bennington, the group's principal songwriters, avoided the tendency to overuse obscenities in their lyrics and concentrated instead on finding the words that would express their anger and vulnerability. "We wanted something people could connect with, not just vulgarity and violence," Bennington explains. Swearing, he says, "seemed like a cheap way to say I'm angry." Shinoda adds, "The one thing we do that's different [from other rap-rock bands] is that we like to keep things a little more introverted, lyrically a little less aggressive."

Although *Hybrid Theory* followed the path established by Limp Bizkit, Papa Roach, Korn, and other "new metal" rap fusion groups (see box on page 82), it managed to create a sound that was unique. The *St. Louis Post-Dispatch* singled out the band's "emotionally charged" vocals, saying that it was not so much *what* they said as *how* they said it that gave the group its unique sound. Against DJ Joe Hahn's electronic backdrop, according to the *Chicago Daily Herald,* there are "menacing guitar riffs, and almost U2-esque underlying keyboard melody, and hip-hop vocals." The *Herald* concluded that Linkin Park is "an up-and-down band. When they get it right, they have an unstoppable power and intensity that recalls the early, more raw melodic metal sounds of the mid-90s, but at their worst they come off as just another Limp Bizkit clone."

Clone or not, the album went on to sell almost eight million copies in the U.S. and 14 million worldwide. It was the best-selling rock album in the country in 2001, crowding out established artists like Britney Spears, Destiny's Child, Alicia Keys, and 'N Sync. At the Billboard Music Awards that year, Linkin Park was named Modern Rock Artist of the Year, and the album was nominated for three Grammy Awards, eventually winning Best Hard Rock Vocal for "Crawling," a song that Delson describes as expressing "those feelings of insecurity and self-doubt that everyone goes through." Members of the band were stunned by their sudden success, which was unprecedented in Warner Brothers history.

"There's a misconception that angry music is going to make someone angry," Delson contends. *"I think it's cathartic, and I think that a lot of kids who do have problems . . . can relate to the lyrics and can go, 'Oh, it's OK to feel that way. I'm not uncool if I feel insecure.'"*

The success of *Hybrid Theory* was tarnished briefly by a tragic incident. Newspaper articles claimed that its music had inspired Andy Williams, a troubled California high school student, to open fire on his classmates in March 2001, killing two students and injuring 13 others. He was a fan of Linkin Park and claimed that songs from their album — especially "One Step Closer," "Papercut," and "In the End" — had given him the courage to carry out his tragic plan. Brad Delson responded to the negative publicity by saying, "There's a misconception that angry music is going to make someone angry. I think it's cathartic, and I think that a lot of kids who do have problems . . . can relate to the lyrics and can go, 'Oh, it's OK to feel that way. I'm not uncool if I feel insecure.'"

Linkin Park followed up their hit debut album by recording "Point of Authority" for the soundtrack for the film *Little Nicky* starring Adam

Sandler, Reese Witherspoon, and Harvey Keitel. The band also released a DVD based on digital video footage from the concert tour they made after the album's release.

Reanimation

The band's next release, *Reanimation* (2002), quickly became controversial. Instead of putting together a second album of new songs, they issued *Reanimation*, a remix version of *Hybrid Theory*. Their goal wasn't just to give their existing songs a new spin. Instead, they wanted to reinterpret the songs with the help of other, and not necessarily well-known, hip-hop artists, record producers, and dance music DJs. *Entertainment Weekly* described the album as "a hostile rap takeover of *Hybrid Theory* rather than a modest recasting of its songs. The drums, vocals, and bludgeoning air-blast guitars of the original recordings are thrown out and replaced by hip-hop minimalism — rumbling pianos, scratchy beats, air-raid-siren effects, and newly recorded raps by lesser-known rhymers." They also pointed out that the remixes "at times obliterate one of the band's most distinctive characteristics — the vocal interplay between singer Chester Bennington and MC Mike Shinoda." Shinoda said they did it for their fans, not for the increased record sales. "We want them to know they can look to us to mix different things together."

The critics' response to *Reanimation* was far from positive, but most agreed that it was an interesting effort. The reviewer for *USA Today* said, "The ambitious remix project succeeds in recasting the band's crunchy rockers with techno and hip-hop treatments but fails to improve on the originals, raising the question: Why bother?" But the reviewer went on to admit that "the resulting patchwork of radical tweaks by skilled understudies has a fresh allure." *Entertainment Weekly* suggested that despite the band's claim that they wanted to expand the limits of rap-rock, perhaps they just weren't ready for a whole new album and needed time to re-charge their creative batteries. *Rolling Stone* agreed that "It's not so much an album as it is a capital-P project, the kind of record that rock stars make when they get caught short of new material between albums."

Meteora

Linkin Park's second album of original songs was released in March 2003. They called it *Meteora,* after a group of monasteries that are clustered on top of a huge rock formation in central Greece. Bennington says that he and Shinoda wanted to write songs that reflected the energy symbolized by the name, which means "hovering in air."

Many in the music industry believe that a jinx is often associated with a successful group's second album. To avoid that sophomore slump, Linkin

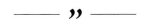

"We definitely have one of the strongest, if not the strongest, fan bases around," Bennington boasts. *"We go from city to city, and we see the same faces over and over again. . . . A lot of bands neglect the fact that the reason they're able to tour and sell T-shirts is because of the kids. It amazes me to see the bands that take their fans for granted. They forget who got them there."*

Park took their time making *Meteora.* They wrote 80 songs before selecting the 12 that would appear on the album and labored for two years on "Somewhere I Belong," the album's first single. Shinoda believes that the result proves the band has grown up. "The first album has feelings of confusion and anger and paranoia," he explains. "We were writing about those from the perspective of young 20-year-old guys." The new album, he says, features songs that express more hope and optimism. It also experiments with different tempos. Songs like "Breaking the Habit" and "Faint" are much faster, while "Easier to Run" is much slower than their earlier songs.

Meteora entered the national pop chart at No. 1 a week after it first appeared in record stores and sold more than 800,000 copies its first week—twice as many as Celine Dion's new album, *One Heart*. But once again, praise was muted from critics who said that the band wasn't doing anything that was really new. The Fort Worth *Star Telegram* accused Linkin Park of "constantly rewriting the same basic song (loud intro, quiet verses, enormous choruses, Chester Bennington screaming his head off) over and over." *Rolling Stone* gave a more balanced appraisal when it said that "the band manages to squeeze the last remaining life out of this nearly extinct [rap-rock] formula with volatile performances and meticulous editing," pointing out that "the band's improved songwriting makes *Meteora* more than yet another remix of its predecessor." The band's fans agreed, and by October 2003 the album had sold more than three million copies.

Connecting with Fans

Perhaps one explanation for Linkin Park's unprecedented success is the importance they attach to spending time with their audience. It is routine for members of the band to walk into the crowd after performances and sign autographs for hours. "We definitely have one of the strongest, if not *the* strongest, fan bases around," Bennington says. "We go from city to city, and we see the same faces over and over again. . . . A lot of bands neglect the fact that the reason they're able to tour and sell T-shirts is because of the kids. It amazes me to see the bands that take their fans for granted. They forget who got them there."

The suddenness of their success has led to rumors that the band is "manufactured"—in other words, that they are the creation of marketing and publicity professionals rather than talented individuals in their own right. "That's the most deeply offensive thing that anyone can say about this band," Bennington comments. "I don't have to explain the way we work, how hard we've battled every step of the way to get heard, how much of the actual success of this band is down to what we've done with our fans and the relationship we've built up with people [who are] into our music."

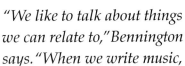

"We like to talk about things we can relate to," Bennington says. "When we write music, there has to be honesty in it. We're trying to say, 'I've gone through this, and we know other people are, too.'"

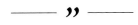

There is no disputing the fact that Linkin Park's lyrics and melodies set them apart from the angry lashing-out of other rap-metal groups. "We like to talk about things we can relate to," Bennington says. "When we write music, there has to be honesty in it. We're trying to say, 'I've gone through this, and we know other people are, too.'"

LIFE AT HOME

Now in their late 20s, the members of Linkin Park have settled down and lead relatively quiet lives when they aren't on tour. Hahn and Bourdon have steady girlfriends, while Bennington, Shinoda, and Farrell are married. Bennington and his wife Samantha had their first child, a son named Draven, in May 2002.

MAJOR INFLUENCES

Perhaps no group has had more influence on Linkin Park than The Deftones, with whom they have admitted a "hero-worship relationship." They have also been influenced by Depeche Mode, a group that managed

Linkn Park poses with their 2002 Grammy Award after winning for Best Hard Rock Performance for "Crawling."

to bridge the gap between the rock and pop worlds. "When I was a kid," Bennington says, "I used to have a recurring dream that Depeche Mode flew a jet into my schoolyard and asked me to be their fifth member. . . . So we performed a concert in front of my school mates and then we flew off on the jet and did a world tour together."

RECORDINGS

Hybrid Theory, 2000
Reanimation, 2002
Meteora, 2003
Live in Texas, 2003

HONORS AND AWARDS

Billboard Music Awards: 2001, Modern Rock Artist of the Year
MTV Music Video Award: 2002, Best Rock Video, for "In the End"
Grammy Award: 2002, Best Hard Rock Vocal, for "Crawling"

FURTHER READING

Periodicals

Billboard, Apr. 5, 2003, p.1
Current Biography Yearbook, 2002
Detroit Free Press, Feb. 3, 2002, p.E1
Guardian (London), Mar. 21, 2003, p.6
New York Post, Mar. 21, 2003, p.66
Philadelphia Inquirer, Mar. 30, 2003, p.H1
Rolling Stone, Mar. 14, 2002, p.42
Time, Jan. 28, 2002, p.52
USA Weekend, July 11-13, 2003, p.6

Online Articles

http://www.nyrock.com/interviews/2003/linkin_int.asp
   (*NY Rock,* "Interview with Mike Shinoda of Linkin Park," May 2003)

ADDRESS

Linkin Park
Warner Bros. Records
3300 Warner Boulevard
Burbank, CA 91505

WORLD WIDE WEB SITES

http://www.linkinpark.com
http://www.mtv.com

Irene D. Long 1951-

American Aerospace Physician and Administrator
First Female Chief Medical Officer of NASA's
Kennedy Space Center

BIRTH

Irene D. Long was born Irene Duhart on November 16, 1951,
in Cleveland, Ohio. Her father, Andrew Duhart, was a steel-
worker who was interested in planes and space travel. Her
mother, Heloweise Davis Duhart, was a teacher of adult education. Long is the second of two children. Her older brother
is a freelance artist.

YOUTH

Long was fascinated with medicine from a young age. She was just three years old when she saw an operation on television. She watched the open-heart surgery and decided it was something she wanted to do. She also had an interest in aviation and space. She was lucky to be growing up at the beginning of the era of space exploration.

When Long was young, in the 1950s and 1960s, the United States was in the middle of the "space race" with the Soviet Union (U.S.S.R.). After the end of World War II in 1945, the U.S. and the U.S.S.R. became rivals as the two countries emerged as the only world superpowers. These two nations became locked in the conflict known as the Cold War—a war defined not by open warfare, but by escalating hostilities between the two nations. The Cold War was also characterized by the division of the major world governments into pro-U.S. and pro-Soviet nations. With the Cold War raging, the two superpowers began what was known as the "arms race," in which the two nations were engaged in a potentially deadly competition to create ever more powerful weapons. The arms race led to the "space race," with the goal to be the first nation to land a man on the moon. Both the U.S.S.R. and the U.S. had the rocket technology necessary to place an orbiting vehicle into space —in fact they had developed that technology as part of weapons delivery systems used in World War II.

Long recalls the precise moment she discovered her dream. "I was watching a show on television called 'Man and the Challenge.' It was about getting ready for human spaceflight. There was a Lieutenant Colonel John Paul Stapp on the show, and it showed him working with sled tests and other research that they were doing at the time. I remember watching the credits, which showed that Lt. Col. Stapp was an Air Force physician specializing in aviation medicine, and I said to myself, 'Wow, that looks like fun.'"

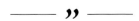

The modern age of space exploration began in 1957 when the Soviet Union launched *Sputnik I*, the first satellite sent into space. The United States became determined to beat the Russians in developing its space program. In 1958, the United States founded the National Aeronautics and Space Administration (NASA). Three years later, President John F. Kennedy announced America's plans to send the first men to the moon. Astronauts and space exploration were in the news and on television.

Long recalls the precise moment she discovered her dream. "I was watching a show on television called 'Man and the Challenge.' It was about getting ready for human spaceflight. There was a Lieutenant Colonel John Paul Stapp on the show, and it showed him working with sled tests and other research that they were doing at the time. I remember watching the credits, which showed that Lt. Col. Stapp was an Air Force physician specializing in aviation medicine, and I said to myself, 'Wow, that looks like fun.'" Long was just nine years old when she told her parents that she wanted to be an aerospace physician when she grew up.

——— " ———

"My parents always gave me the impression that you could do whatever you set your mind to, and that the future depends upon how hard you work and how determined you are."

——— " ———

Long's upbringing inspired her in her dreams. She grew up in the Cleveland area, not far from NASA's Lewis Research Center (now called the John H. Glenn Research Center at Lewis Field). Her father was interested in flying and she sometimes tagged along on his flying lessons. Long's mother and father supported their daughter's plans. "My parents always gave me the impression that you could do whatever you set your mind to, and that the future depends upon how hard you work and how determined you are." Although some people believed that science wasn't a suitable field for an African-American woman, Long never let prejudice keep her from her goals.

EDUCATION

After graduating from East High School in Cleveland, Long tailored her education to her goals. She studied biology at Northwestern University in Chicago and received her bachelor's degree in 1973.

Becoming a doctor requires many years of training. After completing four years of college, students must then attend four years of medical school. At the end of medical school, new doctors decide what field of medicine they wish to practice. Then they complete a "residency" of at least three years in that field. Long entered the St. Louis School of Medicine and earned a medical degree (M.D.) in 1977. She followed this with residency training at the Cleveland Clinic and Mt. Sinai Hospital in Cleveland. She studied general surgery during this period of specialized training.

Long continued her education by accepting another residency at the Wright State University in Dayton, Ohio. This was a very specialized program in aerospace medicine that only accepted a few students each year. Long earned a master's degree in aerospace medicine through this residency. Her studies also included some time at NASA's Ames Research Center in California. There she continued researching the effects of space on the human body. She also got the chance to meet an inspiring figure, Colonel Charles Bolden, one of NASA's first African-American astronauts. "I went to hear him speak and I passed a note to the person who was in charge saying that I was working in an aerospace medicine residency program and I'd like to meet him. After his speech he came over and talked to me and listened to my goals and aspirations and said, 'You look like you'd be a nice person to work for NASA.'"

CAREER HIGHLIGHTS

Important Research into Sickle-Cell Anemia

Part of Long's special medical training included doing medical research. In 1982 she published an important research paper about the sickle-cell trait. Sickle-cell anemia is a genetic disease that affects red blood cells. Normal red blood cells are round, like doughnuts, and carry oxygen to the cells of the body. In people with sickle-cell anemia, the red blood cells can change into a crescent shape, like a sickle. This change happens when the cell gives up its oxygen. When many cells form the sickle shape, blood clots can form. This can lead to great pain or even a dangerous stroke, when a clot blocks an important blood vessel.

Sickle-cell anemia is genetic disease, meaning that you inherit it from your parents. If both parents pass you the sickle-cell gene, you have sickle-cell disease. If only one parent passes the sickle-cell gene to you, you have sickle-cell trait. The sickle-cell gene is particularly common among African-Americans, with 1 in 12 carrying the trait and 1 in 375 having sickle-cell disease, but people of any race or ethnic background can have the disease.

Long's research paper addressed the potential dangers of flying for people with the sickle-cell trait. Sickle-cells are formed when there is a shortage of oxygen in the blood. Situations that deprive the body of oxygen can cause painful attacks. These conditions include too much exercise, too much cold, and high-altitude flying. Long showed in her article that the reduced oxygen level in a plane will not affect people with the sickle-cell trait. This

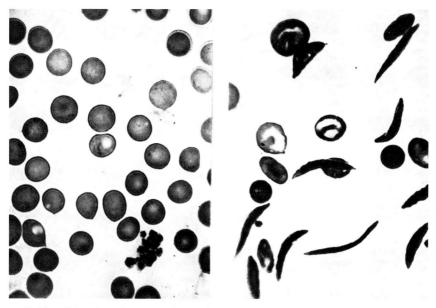

Sickle cell is a hereditary condition that involves the red blood cells that carry oxygen throughout the body. In these photos, the cells at left are in their normal round shape and the cells at right are deformed by sickle cell disease.

research helped reassure people with sickle-cell trait that flying posed no danger to them.

Achieving a Dream

Long spent many years preparing for a job as an aerospace physician. In 1982 she realized her dream when she joined the medical staff at NASA's Kennedy Space Center in Florida. One of her first duties was to help staff the biomedical consoles in the Launch Control Center. Her job was to monitor the heart rates and blood pressure of the astronauts to make sure they were safe to launch. She was on duty on January 28, 1986, the day the space shuttle *Challenger* exploded shortly after takeoff, killing everyone on board. On that day it was her job to make sure staff doctors, rescue teams, and local hospitals were ready for any possibility. "We had to be ready to provide emergency support in a situation where it was extremely difficult to know what was happening."

Shortly after joining the Kennedy Space Center staff, Long was chosen to head their Occupational Medicine and Environmental Health Office. She became the first African-American woman in this position. During her time as Chief of the Occupational Medicine and Environmental Health Office, Long oversaw a staff of more than 200 doctors, nurses, and environmental health specialists. Overall, she was responsible for the safety of the more than 18,000 people working at the Center.

Long and her staff had many responsibilities. They had to provide medical treatment in case of an emergency on the ground. All space launches, whether of rockets or the space shuttle, can be dangerous. There is the potential for fires, explosions, and exposure to toxic chemicals. All of these events could endanger many workers on the ground. There are also special dangers the astronauts face, such as decompression. This happens when there is a sudden change in air pressure in the cabin of the ship. Changes in air pressure can affect how blood works in the body, so people suffering from decompression need specialized medical treatment. Long's office had to be ready for these and other types of emergencies.

At NASA's Kennedy Space Center in Florida, Long helped staff the biomedical consoles in the Launch Control Center. She was on duty on January 28, 1986, when the space shuttle **Challenger** *exploded shortly after takeoff, killing everyone on board. "We had to be ready to provide emergency support in a situation where it was extremely difficult to know what was happening."*

Another duty of Long and her staff was to make sure that all areas in the Kennedy Space Center were safe for the workers. In addition to the launch area, there are many other areas that needed to be inspected for safety issues. People working with rocket fuels needed to be protected from explosions. The Kennedy Space Center tests how tools work in space by using

them underwater, and divers in these programs needed protection as well. People working with toxic chemicals needed a place safe from fumes. Long set up a Toxic Substance Registry System to keep track of these potential dangers. The workplace safety program Long directed was so thorough it has been a model for many companies and industries.

A final responsibility of Long and her staff was to give physicals to employees at the Space Center. Many jobs at NASA are physically demanding or potentially dangerous. Long's office made sure that the employees were both healthy and able to perform their duties. They also investigated how living in space affects an astronaut's body. Their research included experiments in the lab and careful observations of the astronauts' physical state, both before and after space flights.

Preparing for Life in Space

In 1994, Long became Director of the Kennedy Space Center's Biomedical Office. Her duties included program management of the center's programs in aerospace and occupational medicine, life sciences research, and environmental health. She was also responsible for the operations management of the life sciences support facilities. Part of her job became working on the development of the International Space Station (ISS).

The Kennedy Space Center does more than just send the space shuttle on missions. It also helps plan for America's involvement in the International Space Station, which is considered a scientific and engineering marvel. The International Space Station is in orbit in space, 220 miles above the earth, where there is very little gravity. It is a permanent human outpost in space that has been inhabited since November 2000 by crews from the United States, Russia, Canada, Japan, and several European countries. The ISS is gradually being built in space — modules are built on earth and then transported into space, where they are assembled by the astronauts. The astronauts do some of the assembly on spacewalks, and they also use a robotic arm and crane, which arrived on an early flight. A series of continuing space flights are delivering additional components, as well as food and other supplies for the crew members. When completed, the ISS will have room for up to seven astronauts and will house six separate research laboratories. Astronauts and cosmonauts are already living and working on the station in rotating crews, each staying up to six months. They perform scientific research that may one day allow humans to live in space permanently. Crew return vehicles will remain attached to the ISS, ready for use in the event of an emergency.

At this point, there is one crucial barrier to humans' ability to live permanently in space: humans will not be able to colonize space until they can supply their own food and water. But there is no room on a space station for agricultural fields. The moon and Mars have no healthy soil or sources of water. Under Long's direction, the space center's Controlled Ecological Life Support System (CELSS) project explored ways to grow food without soil. An important goal was for food production to be *bioregenerative*, meaning self-sustaining. This means that everything used to grow food, from the water to the air to the fertilizer, needs to be recycled. Even waste products on a space station would be used to grow food.

The Controlled Environment Life Support System (CELSS), set up in a self-contained bubble in an old hangar, has explored ways to produce food, water, and oxygen and reduce carbon dioxide.

Working in an old hangar, the CELSS team set up a self-contained, bubble-shaped station called the Biomass Production Chamber. Their experiments with bioregeneration have produced important crops, including wheat, soybeans, potatoes, tomatoes, and lettuce. They also helped generate purified water and air. People breathe in oxygen and breathe out carbon dioxide. Too much carbon dioxide is poisonous to humans. The crops in the CELSS experiment produced oxygen that people could breathe and reduced carbon dioxide levels before they became poisonous. Long is proud of the efforts of CELSS and her environmental and safety staffs. "I would like to think that we are pioneers in occupational medicine for the space program. What we're doing here now on the ground will someday be done in space, be it on a space station, the moon, or Mars."

Long is proud of the efforts of CELSS and her environmental and safety staffs. "I would like to think that we are pioneers in occupational medicine for the space program. What we're doing here now on the ground will someday be done in space, be it on a space station, the moon, or Mars."

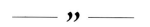

Becoming NASA's First Female Chief Medical Officer

In 2000, Long became the first minority woman to achieve the civilian equivalent of a general's rank at Kennedy Space Center. That year she was named Chief Medical Officer and Associate Director of Spaceport Services. This also made her the Center's first female Chief Medical Officer. Her job in this position was to coordinate health and safety efforts throughout the entire Kennedy Space Center. This included planning for the Center's future needs and developing ways to prevent environmental and health problems before they happen.

As Associate Director of Spaceport Services, Long helps the Kennedy Space Center prepare for the future of space travel. Their goal is to make space travel safer, faster, and cheaper, so that space travel may some day be as common as air travel. They look at ways to make space launches and the delivery of space cargo more efficient. They try to improve procedures with new computer systems and new technologies. Long's efforts in this department are another way she works toward achieving the dream of a permanent human habitat in space.

Working in the Community

Throughout her career at NASA, Long has also been involved in outreach programs. In 1985 she helped start the Space Life Sciences Training

Program at Kennedy Space Center. This program encourages women and minority college students to explore careers in science. College students join the program and spend six weeks with the scientists at Kennedy Space Center. They learn about space physiology, or how the human body functions in space. They also study how space affects plants and animals. They learn to plan experiments and work as a team. A whole generation of students have now been inspired by this opportunity.

Long has also spread her knowledge through teaching and membership in professional organizations. She has taught about community health at the Wright State University School of Medicine. She is a member of the Society of NASA Flight Surgeons and served as that group's president in 1999. She also belongs to the Aerospace Medical Association and its Space Medicine Branch. These organizations and others have recognized her hard work. In 1986 she received the Kennedy Space Center's Federal Woman of the Year Award; in 1995 the Society of NASA Flight Surgeons gave Long their Presidential Award; in 1998 she earned an Outstanding Achievement Award from Women in Aerospace; and in 2001 she was named to the Ohio Women's Hall of Fame.

——— " ———

Long knows that because of her success, she is now a role model for others. "I hope that I am someone that people can look at and say, 'I can do that too.'" She has made her dreams come true through hard work and persistence. "I made it happen," she said. "Every time someone told me I couldn't do something, I went out and did it."

——— " ———

Long knows that because of her success, she is now a role model for others. "I hope that I am someone that people can look at and say, 'I can do that too.'" She has made her dreams come true through hard work and persistence. "I *made* it happen," she said. "Every time someone told me I couldn't do something, I went out and did it." Her message to those who would follow her is to set goals and work hard to achieve them. "There's a saying that to know where you're going, you must know where you've been. I think it's just as important to say, to succeed and prosper in the present, you must know where you're headed."

HOME AND FAMILY

Long is single and lives in Merritt Island, Florida. She enjoys reading, cooking, and entertaining friends.

HOBBIES AND OTHER INTERESTS

Long has enjoyed creative craft projects since she was a little girl. She creates and sometimes sells her own flower wreaths. She also makes hand-made lotions and soaps using homegrown herbs and plants. She collects antiques, including antique furniture and glassware. She also enjoys collecting dolls and doll house miniatures, and makes her own miniature furniture. She is involved in her community, serving on the board of directors of Crosswinds Youth Services. She is also a member of the National Association for the Advancement of Colored People (NAACP).

HONORS AND AWARDS

Federal Woman of the Year Award (Kennedy Space Center): 1986
Presidential Award (Society of NASA Flight Surgeons): 1995
Outstanding Achievement Award (Women in Aerospace): 1998
Named to Ohio Women's Hall of Fame: 2001

FURTHER READING

Books

Burns, Khephra, and William Miles. *Black Stars in Orbit: NASA's African American Astronauts*, 1995
Encyclopedia of World Biography, 1998
Notable Scientists: From 1900 to the Present, 2001
Notable Twentieth-Century Scientists, 1995
Webster, Raymond B. *African-American Firsts in Science and Technology*, 2000

Periodicals

Ebony, Sep. 1984, p.61
Florida Today, Aug. 23, 2000, p.1

Online Articles

http://www-pao.ksc.nasa.gov/release/1994/87-94.htm
  (*Kennedy Space Center*, "NASA News Release Online," Aug. 1, 1994)
http://www.scinfo.org/sicklept.htm
  (*The Sickle Cell Information Center*, "What Is Sickle Cell Anemia," Apr. 6, 2002)
http://medschool.slu.edu/oma/newsletter/march97.pdf
  (*The Supplemental Instructor, Saint Louis University School of Medicine*, "Physician of Color Highlight," Mar. 1997)

Online Databases

Biography Resource Center Online, 2003, articles from *Encyclopedia of World Biography*, 2001, and *Notable Scientists: From 1900 to the Present*, 2001

ADDRESS

Dr. Irene D. Long
NASA Kennedy Space Center
Chief Medical Officer
Kennedy Space Center, FL 32899

WORLD WIDE WEB SITES

http://www-pao.ksc.nasa.gov/bios/long.htm
http://www.ksc.nasa.gov
http://www.nasa.gov

Mandy Moore 1984-

American Singer and Actress
Creator of the Hit Songs "Candy," "Crush," "In My
Pocket," and "Walk Me Home," and Star of the
Movies *A Walk to Remember* and *How to Deal*

BIRTH

Amanda Leigh Moore, who prefers to be called Mandy, was
born on April 10, 1984, in Nashua, New Hampshire. She is the
daughter of Don Moore, a commercial airline pilot for American Airlines, and Stacy Moore, a former journalist for the

Orlando Sentinel. Moore has two brothers: Scott, who is two years older, and Kyle, who is three years younger.

YOUTH

Mandy Moore was an entertainer in the making from the time she was a very young girl. Yet if her family had remained in New Hampshire, she might not have blossomed the way she did. But her parents moved the family to Orlando, Florida, when she was two months old. Orlando is the home of Disney World and many other tourist attractions, and by the early 1990s it was becoming a training ground for many of today's pop entertainers, including Britney Spears, Justin Timberlake, and Christina Aguilera. It was a much better place for a young entertainer to be discovered than the little city of Nashua.

However, it wasn't the pop scene that first attracted Moore; it was Broadway musicals. When she was just six years old, her parents took her to see a student performance of the Broadway hit *Oklahoma!* From that moment on, Moore knew what she wanted to do with her life: she wanted to become a singer, preferably in musical theater. She told her parents that she wanted to be a singer, but they thought it was just a phase. Nevertheless, they agreed to pay for some voice lessons; eventually, they became convinced she was serious. "When I was about nine my parents realized that I really wanted to perform, that it wasn't a phase. From then on all I did was appear in community theater shows. If anyone needed a little girl [in the cast], I was the one."

Moore also acted in school plays and with the Civic Kids troupe, which was part of the Civic Theatre of Central Florida. "I knew I wanted to have the lead in the sixth-grade play, and when I got to sixth grade, sure enough, I got the lead and was on stage performing, and that sealed the deal." Moore appeared in such shows as *South Pacific,* which was her first play, *Guys and Dolls, The Sound of Music, Bye Bye Birdie,* and *A Christmas Carol.*

FIRST JOBS

Moore's career took off very early. By the time she was just nine years old, her parents had arranged for her to perform the national anthem in front of more than 10,000 people at an Orlando Magic basketball game. Soon she was also performing at other sporting events and became known in Orlando as "The National Anthem Girl." When she was 11, her parents hired a professional talent agent, and she began finding small jobs on television, especially for Nickelodeon and Disney doing voice-overs for cartoons (providing voices for animated characters). Her first movie "role," in fact, was as the voice of Ducky in the dinosaur movie *The Land Before Time*.

It was while singing the title song for what she described as "a corny kids' cartoon show about sea turtles" that she was "discovered" at the age of 14. A Federal Express delivery man named Victor Cade, who worked as a part-time talent scout, heard her sing at a recording session and thought Moore had real talent. Without telling the young singer, he approached her parents and asked if they would give him a tape that he could mail to his friend at Sony Records, Dave McPherson. Figuring that it was worth a shot, they agreed. McPherson forwarded the demo tape to Epic/550 Records (part of Sony Records), and the executives there loved it. Moore was called in to audition, and within a week she had signed a recording contract.

"I had to leave school in December to start recording," Moore said about earning her first recording contract, "so I had to tell my teachers that I got a record deal. It was so unheard of, and they didn't take it seriously. They just said, 'Okay, Sweetie, see you next semester. Make sure you finish your homework. Have a Merry Christmas.' But I didn't go back. Since then, everything has fit together like a nice little puzzle."

EDUCATION

The life of an up-and-coming singing star leaves little time for a traditional education. This was certainly true for Moore, who left Bishop Moore Catholic High School halfway through her freshman year, when she was working on her first record. "I had to leave school in December to start recording," she recalled, "so I had to tell my teachers that I got a record deal. It was so unheard of, and they didn't take it seriously. They just said, 'Okay, Sweetie, see you next semester. Make sure you finish your homework. Have a Merry Christmas.' But I didn't go back. Since then, everything has fit together like a nice little puzzle." Moore still stays close to two or three friends she made while in high school.

Although she doesn't have the opportunity to experience the social aspects of attending school, Moore is determined to get an education. She has been taking correspondence courses through Texas Tech University and the University of Nebraska. "I have a tutor back home," she explained. "When traveling I do it any time I can. I do my schoolwork on the Internet;

it's the most convenient. I want to go to college and study journalism. Even if I don't use it, I want to have it to fall back on. My mom was a journalist. I love to write. I guess it's in my blood." In addition to her regular schooling, Moore has also had some formal acting training; she attended the performing academy Stagedoor Manor for two summers.

> "My music is pop but with an edge. Every song is different on the album. Some have an R&B edge, some have a rock edge, some have a dance edge. It's not just bubble-gum pop music. I think it's good to have a little variety and not just keep giving people the same thing over and over."

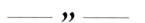

CAREER HIGHLIGHTS

Creating a Star

Moore got her start working for Epic/550 Records. From the beginning, executives knew that she had a lot of raw talent. But how to construct a career from that talent was the big question, one that Moore has been working on ever since she signed her first contract. To get the word out about the new singer, the music company created two Web sites on the Internet dedicated to her. The strategy worked, and soon young Web surfers were beginning to buzz about this new musical find. Next, Moore was set up as an opening act for the popular boy bands 'N Sync and The Backstreet Boys, and in the summer of 1999 she went on a tour with them. "I learned everything from being on tour with the Backstreet Boys," she said. "They're inspirational to me, because they're so down-to-earth and nothing has fazed them. All the success they've had hasn't changed them a bit. And 'N Sync was exactly the same."

Now that she was developing a fan base, it was time to get her first album out. Still only 15 years old, Moore herself couldn't believe she was actually going to record a CD. "It's really surreal. I thought a record company would sign an artist my age and wait until I was 17 or 18 before they started having me do stuff. But I just jumped right in." The songs for her first CD, *So Real*, were mostly written by Shaun Fisher and Tony Battaglia. Though Moore didn't have much say in the contents of her first CD, she liked the results. As she said in 1999, when *So Real* was released, "My music is pop but with an edge. Every song is different on the album. Some have an R&B edge, some have a rock edge, some have a dance edge. It's not just bubble-gum pop music. I think it's good to have a little variety and not just keep

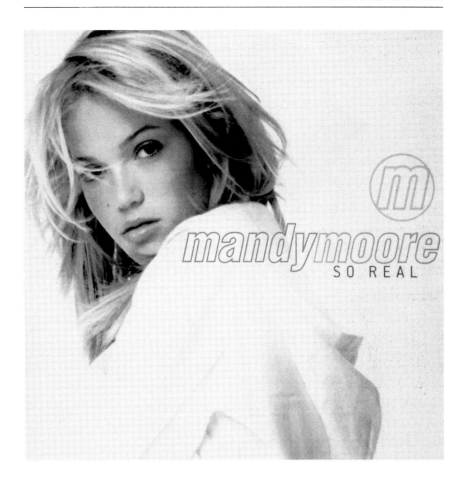

giving people the same thing over and over." The first single to be released was "Candy," and Moore got a big thrill when she heard it played on the radio. "It is the trippiest thing in the whole world just to [hear], 'And here's 'Candy' by Mandy Moore.' It's like, oh my gosh, it's a feeling you can never get used to. And it's a feeling that's so, so indescribable."

First CDs and MTV

So Real and "Candy" were released in 1999. Although they didn't skyrocket to the top of the charts, it wasn't long before *So Real* had sold over a million copies, making it a platinum record. By the next year, things were happening fast for Moore. She became a commercial spokesperson and model for the skin care line Neutrogena and the clothing designer Tommy Hilfiger, and she made several appearances on TV specials and on the

MTV show "Total Request Live" (TRL). Then, in 2000, she hosted her own program called "The Mandy Moore Show," in which she played videos and offered advice to teens. With her popularity soaring, she was voted one of "The Hottest Stars under 25" in *Teen People* magazine. With the success of *So Real,* her producers realized they had a new hot singer on their hands. To keep her in the spotlight, they quickly released a second album.

I Wanna Be with You (2000), Moore's follow-up release, includes remixes of songs from *So Real,* as well as several new songs. The second album went platinum, too; the title track became part of the soundtrack to the movie *Center Stage,* and sales of the album as a whole did even better than her debut CD. Even though only a year separates these first two albums, Moore and the managers at her record company felt the young singer had matured in that short time. "We had recorded a couple of these new tracks," she recalled about the time they were preparing the second CD, "thinking they would be for the next album, without even telling the label. My manager went in and played them for the record company. They were like, 'Who is this?' You can see there's a far cry between 'Candy' and 'I Wanna Be with You,' and there's more where that came from. I think it's a great transition." Some critics found the revamped record to be better than the original. "It doesn't stretch the teen pop formula much, just enough to give the record character. . . . Moore delivers the songs sturdily, never taking the forefront, but blending into the lush layered production, so the music just rolls forth as a whole," Thomas Erlewine wrote in *All Music Guide*. But many others were not as enthusiastic, including reviewer Cameron Adams. "Supplied with a bunch of love songs probably written by people twice her age, [Moore] sings them with all the conviction of a girl who is more likely to play with toys than boys. But the main problem here is that while Britney gets to work with the A-list of songwriters and producers, Mandy's songs really aren't all that good. . . . It's McMusic."

For Moore's third album, **Mandy Moore,** *she said, "It's so cool to have more creative control on what songs are on it and who I work with. That makes everything a little bit more personal."*

Moore's third album, the self-titled *Mandy Moore,* was released in 2001. With this CD, the singer had some clout with the studio, and she was able to write and perform a number of her own songs. For Moore, it marked a departure from her previous recordings. "I'm older, I'm not the same girl. That's why I wanted this album to be self-titled. For the first time, I really feel the music is a reflection of me. . . . I recorded the first album when I was just 14. I was excited just to be in the studio doing my own album, I wasn't concerned with the material." The first song Moore wrote for the album, the acoustic number "When I Talk to You," is not the usual love song. "It's not a song about romance, which is kind of cool," she commented. "It's so cool to have more creative control on what songs are on it and who I work with. That makes everything a little bit more personal."

Critics noted an improvement on this new CD. The album, overall, was called a bit more sophisticated than her previous efforts, with more advanced musical arrangements. According to the review on MTV.com, "Mandy Moore is stylistically confident enough to venture into sonic areas beyond the usual Aguilera/Spears axis. For one thing, there's more of a pronounced R&B flavor to Moore's songs than those of her contemporaries. The production takes more chances as well, as witnessed by the exotic textures that open the lush 'Saturate Me' and 'One Sided Love.'" And *Rolling Stone* reviewer Barry Walters went so far as to call *Mandy Moore* "the most startlingly liberated teen pop since [the] eighties." "With this album," said reviewer Nekesa Mumbi Moody, "Moore is slowly moving from a teen pop starlet into a credible adult pop singer."

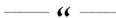

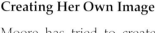

"The only thing I have in common with Britney or Jessica or Christina is the fact that we're all close in age. We all make fairly different-sounding records. As blessed as I feel to be working in this industry, it's frustrating to sometimes feel discounted or negatively judged because of superficial elements and not because of my actual work."

Creating Her Own Image

Moore has tried to create her own image as a singer. At first, she was often compared to other teen entertainers like Britney Spears, Christina Aguilera, and Jessica Simpson. Moore, however, sees significant differences between her and these other stars. Comparing herself to Spears, for example, she noted that her music is different and that she doesn't emphasize dancing as much in her performances: "I think as people pay attention, they can see we're pursuing different directions," she said in 2002. "I have a seven-piece band, and that's all. We don't use any recorded tracks, and I don't bring any dancers [to stage shows]. I don't dance. On my first video they had me dancing, and then they looked and said, 'Hmm, maybe Mandy shouldn't dance.'" In general, she doesn't like being categorized with the other singers who preceded her. "The only thing I have in common with Britney or Jessica or Christina is the fact that we're all close in age. We all make fairly different-sounding records. As blessed as I feel to be working in this industry, it's frustrating to sometimes feel discounted or negatively judged because of superficial elements and not because of my actual work."

Moore has also tried to create her own image as an actress. She turned down a role in the popular television series "Dawson's Creek" because, as she said, "the part was a little bit too old for me; it was a little too risqué." She has been equally careful when selecting parts for movies. Her first big role was in the 2001 G-rated Disney film *The Princess Diaries*, based on the

*Heather Matarazzo, Anne Hathaway, and Mandy Moore (left to right)
on the set of* The Princess Diaries.

novel of the same name by Meg Cabot (for more information on Cabot,
see *Biography Today Authors*, Vol. 12). The movie was directed by Garry
Marshall and starred Julie Andrews, Anne Hathaway, and Heather Matarazzo. In the movie, Mia (played by Anne Hathaway), is a high school out-
cast who discovers she is actually the princess of a small country in Europe.
Moore plays Mia's nemesis, Lana, who is a nasty socialite cheerleader.
Although she auditioned for the part and won the role just as any professional actress might, Moore still felt a bit awkward at first. "I was intimidat-
ed, like, the first day going to the set," she admitted. "I mean, here I am,
I'm like this singer, and I'm going to the set working with Garry Marshall
and all these other professional actors—Julie Andrews—that really
freaked me out!" *The Princess Diaries*, though not a blockbuster, generally
did well in theaters and proved to be a big success with the teen audience,
particularly the many fans of Cabot's novels.

A Walk to Remember

Next up for Moore was her biggest acting part yet: the starring role in *A
Walk to Remember* (2002). Based on a novel by Nicholas Sparks, *A Walk to
Remember* co-stars Shane West, Peter Coyote, and Daryl Hannah. Moore
plays Jamie Sullivan, the dowdy daughter of a Baptist minister (Coyote).

113

Moore had her first starring role in
A Walk to Remember,
which also featured Shane West.

Quiet, studious, and oblivious to current fashions, Jamie is not a popular student among her high school peers. So the rebellious Landon Carter (West) is not very happy when she is made his tutor and acting partner in the school. Despite themselves, Jamie and Landon become attracted to each other, and both learn to grow in the process. The twist in the story comes when Landon learns a terrible secret about Jamie.

Some critics found *A Walk to Remember* to be touching and sweet —even a little too sweet and corny. Yet even those who didn't like the film still had good things to say about Moore's acting. For example, *Entertainment Weekly* writer Owen Gleiberman said bluntly that "It wasn't a good movie, yet some of the scenes between Moore and Shane West had a surprising tenderness." And Bob Strauss, the reviewer from the *Guardian,* felt that the movie "ladles even more syrup on the sappy Nicholas Sparks source novel." But he admired her for taking risks with her career in playing a conservative character and noted that *A Walk to Remember* did better at the box office than the Britney Spears movie *Crossroads.* "Moore does really bold stuff," Strauss concluded admiringly. "Moore, just 17, has screen appeal and poise as well," Richard Corliss wrote in *Time* magazine. "When pop-star status deserts her, she might become a movie star, or something more precious: a fine actress."

How to Deal

Moore's second starring role came in the 2003 film *How to Deal,* based on the novels *Someone Like You* and *That Summer* by Sarah Dessen. Moore played Halley Martin, who learns how to deal with a series of misfortunes in her life. Moore felt the character was completely unlike her. Whereas Halley is highly skeptical about the possibility of finding true love, Moore calls herself "a pretty romantic person. . . . I believe in love and falling in love at a young age." Halley, however, has good reasons for being cynical: her parents are breaking up, her sister constantly fights with the man in

Mandy Moore as Halley and Trent Ford as Macon in a scene from How to Deal.

her life, and her best friend is pregnant by her no-good boyfriend. But when Halley meets a similar skeptic named Macon (played by Trent Ford), finding a kindred spirit might lead to unexpected results. Moore has said that she chose the role of Halley because it would test her acting abilities. "I couldn't find two similarities between myself and the character," she commented. "But I think that's why I was so moved to take on a challenge like that. I wanted to get inside her head and figure out why someone who is obviously so loved felt unloved by those around her."

Critical reaction to *How to Deal*, like the reaction to *A Walk to Remember*, was mixed. Reviewers liked Moore's performance better than the movie itself. For example, a *USA Today* writer compared *How to Deal* to "a second-rate TV movie" but felt that "it's good for . . . showcasing the bona fide acting talents of pop singer Mandy Moore." Christian Toto was pleased to see that this "peppy pop singer can act," lamenting only that "Moore's efforts [are] squandered by a hollow script."

Recent Work

As a singer, Moore feels that she's just starting to mature and that her tastes in music are changing. "I've just grown up, and I think that's reflected in every aspect of my life, as an artist and as a person." It might not be surprising, then, that on her 2003 release, *Coverage,* she tries to challenge herself again. The songs on this album were all originally recorded during the 1970s and 1980s by such artists as Carly Simon, Joni Mitchell, Todd Rundgren, Elton John, Cat Stevens, and Joan Armatrading. But on her recordings, Moore rearranges them to fit her own personal style. "I guess I did the record for selfish reasons," she confessed, "because the music that's on the album isn't music I grew up listening to. Back then I was a huge musical-theater fan, and so this album is made up of music I've discovered only over the past two years. I feel like a lot of people my age are kind of missing out on it."

———— **"** ————

"[There] is no greater adrenaline rush than performing live at a concert. You can't duplicate that feeling doing a movie or hosting something on MTV. Live performance is the cream of the crop. It's a love affair, a wonderful cycle. The more an audience gives you, the more you give back."

———— **"** ————

For Moore to tackle songs that had become classics before she was born was a daring step for the young pop singer, according to some music critics. For example, Mim Udovitch of the *International Herald Tribune* wrote that "From one perspective, that kind of risk might be regarded as insane, but from another, it is an intelligent, slightly awkward, and sincere thing to do, the act of someone for whom contrivance has failed and whose strong attachment to music is that of a real 19-year-old young woman." Referring to the frequent comparisons between Moore and such pop singers as Britney Spears, Udovitch added, "If you're going to spend your life and career being compared to other people anyway, why not shoot for the moon?" Other critics were less enthusiastic, as in this comment from Chuck Arnold in *People* magazine: "*[Coverage]* feels like it was a rush job, a quick-and-easy way to get an album done for a girl who was too swamped to spend much time in the studio. . . . Maybe in another 10 to 20 years Moore might possess the interpretive powers to make *Coverage* work. For now, though, it sounds as if a girl was sent to do a woman's job."

As an actress, Moore next appears in the 2004 romantic comedy *Chasing Liberty* as Anna Foster, the 18-year-old daughter of the President of the United States. As the President's only child, Anna is constantly monitored by her parents, Secret Service agents, and the media. Foster just wants to be like any rebellious teenager, with the freedom to live her life without

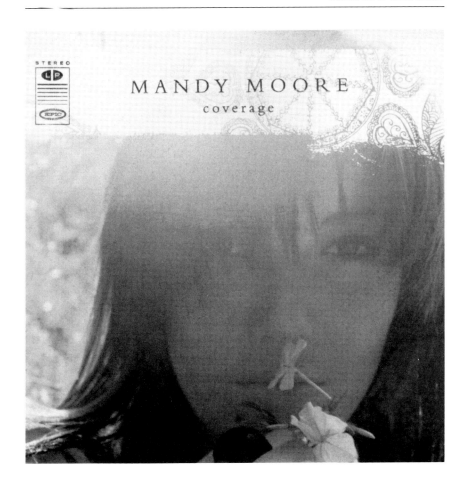

MANDY MOORE
coverage

constant supervision. So while on a diplomatic trip to Europe she escapes and meets a boy (Matthew Goode), who doesn't know who she really is. They set out on a romantic road trip through Europe. But eventually she'll have to head back home — and Anna worries about what will happen when he discovers her real identity. Coincidentally, another movie about the President's daughter — titled *First Daughter* and starring Katie Holmes — will also be released in 2004.

Future Plans

Even though Moore has gained acceptance as an actress, she has said she still prefers singing. "Music is my first love. Acting is like a side career that just kind of took off," she commented. She also once said that "there is no greater adrenaline rush than performing live at a concert. You can't duplicate that feeling doing a movie or hosting something on MTV. Live performance is the cream of the crop. It's a love affair, a wonderful cycle. The more an audience gives you, the more you give back." Moore hopes to have the chance soon to go back on tour. "I want to get back on the road, especially with this music [from *Coverage*]. . . . I just want to be on stage, connecting with an audience, and continue to test my boundaries." Someday, this might take her back to the place where she started: live musical theater. As she once said, "My ultimate goal is to be on Broadway. . . . [Recording albums] has been a dream of mine, to sing my own music and get to perform everywhere. But Broadway is the ultimate thing for me." She added, "My sixth-grade play was *Guys and Dolls*. I got to play Miss Adelaide. That would be my dream role, to play Miss Adelaide on Broadway."

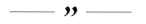

> *"I love my parents,"* Moore proclaimed. *"I have a great family. I have a great relationship [with them]. They've been traveling with me since I was 14 and kind of started in all this madness. And they're great. They keep me sane. My family just keeps me grounded."*

MAJOR INFLUENCES

"I've been influenced by Madonna, Janet Jackson, Bette Middler, and Karen Carpenter," Moore has said, adding that "Karen Carpenter had one of the most beautiful voices in the entire world."

HOME AND FAMILY

Moore spent much of her life in Orlando, Florida, but more recently she purchased a home in Los Feliz, California. She brought her family with her to live in the spacious house because she likes being close to them. "I love my parents," she proclaimed. "I have a great family. I have a great relationship [with them]. They've been traveling with me since I was 14 and kind of started in all this madness. And they're great. They keep me sane. My family just keeps me grounded." Moore, who is single, is currently involved with American tennis star Andy Roddick.

FAVORITE MOVIES AND MUSIC

Moore is a fan of Bette Midler's music and movies. She claims to have seen the movie *Beaches* "at least 20 times," and she also remembers loving Midler's song "The Wind beneath My Wings," which she used to sing on her karaoke machine when she was about nine years old. Besides Midler, she is also a fan of actors Gwyneth Paltrow and Ryan Phillippe. As for music, she enjoys a wide variety of genres. Although she has said she doesn't have a favorite group, she once added: "I'm a huge fan of New Radicals. I'm constantly singing to them." Moore has also listed Norah Jones, Jeff Buckley, and Citizen Cope among her favorites.

HOBBIES AND OTHER INTERESTS

When she's not working, Moore likes to shop, especially on the Internet. "I am such a computer geek," she once confessed. "I couldn't live without the Internet."

RECORDINGS

So Real, 1999
I Wanna Be with You, 2000
Mandy Moore, 2001
Coverage, 2003

CREDITS

Movies

Dr. Dolittle 2, 2001
The Princess Diaries, 2001
A Walk to Remember, 2002
How to Deal, 2003

Other

"The Mandy Moore Show," 2000 (television series)

HONORS AND AWARDS

MTV Movie Award: 2002, for Best Breakthrough Female

FURTHER READING

Books

Bankston, John. *Mandy Moore,* 2002 (juvenile)
Contemporary Musicians, Vol. 35, 2002
Peters, Beth. *Pop Princesses: The Dish behind Today's Hottest Teen Divas,* 2000
    (juvenile)

Periodicals

Billboard, June 10, 2000, p.94; Oct. 21, 2000, p.25

Entertainment Weekly, Aug. 11, 2000, p.85; Feb. 8, 2002, p.51; July 25, 2003, p.50

Girls' Life, June/July 2001, p.42 Feb./Mar. 2002, p.40

Interview, Aug. 2003, p.125

Los Angeles Times, Jan. 5, 2003, p.K1; July 18, 2003, p.E17

New York Times, May 5, 2003, p.C7; July 20, 2003, pp.AR11, E22

People, July 3, 2000, p.110; Dec. 24, 2001, p.27; Feb. 11, 2002, p.31; Mar. 4, 2002, p.59; Feb. 17, 2003, p.24; July 28, 2003, pp.22, 29

Rolling Stone, Mar. 16, 2000, p.23; Oct. 31, 2002, p.81

San Francisco Chronicle, Aug. 6, 2000, p.47; Jan. 20, 2002, p.37; July 28, 2002, p.36

Seventeen, Nov. 2000, p.123; May 2001, p.174; July 2001, p.122

Teen Magazine, Oct. 1999, p.52; Nov. 2000, p.6; Aug. 2001, p.154

Teen People, Feb. 1, 2002, p.110; Sep. 1, 2002, p.124; Aug. 2003, p.242

Time, Feb. 25, 2002, p.62

USA Today, Jan. 25, 2002, p.D11; Jan. 22, 2003, p.C2; July 16, 2003, p.D2; July 18, 2003, p.E4

Washington Post, Jan. 30, 2000, p.G1

Online Databases

Biography Resource Center Online, 2003, article from *Contemporary Musicians,* 2002

ADDRESS

Mandy Moore
Sony — Epic Records
2100 Colorado Avenue
Santa Monica, CA 90404

WORLD WIDE WEB SITES

http://www.mandymoore.com
http://www.mtv.com

Thich Nhat Hanh 1926-

Vietnamese Buddhist Monk
Leading Peace Activist, Respected Teacher of
Buddhism, and Author of Nearly 100 Books

BIRTH

Thich Nhat Hanh was born in October 1926 in central Vietnam, in Southeast Asia. Vietnam is south of China, on a pe-
ninsula near Thailand, Laos, and Cambodia. His father worked
for the Vietnamese government to resettle people from over-
crowded villages to new areas. Nhat Hanh was one of six chil-

dren. His name is pronounced "Tick-Naught-Han" or "Tick-Not-Han." "Thich" is an honorary title, similar to "Reverend," used by Vietnamese Buddhist monks. Nhat Hanh's followers call him "Thay" (pronounced "thai"), which means teacher.

YOUTH

The Buddhist religion has been a central part of Nhat Hanh's life. Buddhism does not center on a person's relationship with a god or gods. Instead, Buddhists focus on rising gradually to a higher spiritual level, by means of ethical, compassionate behavior. Buddhists believe that they can be reincarnated, or brought back to life, in a higher state of existence. The religion is named for its founder, Buddha Shakyamuni, who was born in northern India (now Nepal) in 624 B.C. About 360 million people worldwide practice Buddhism.

Nhat Hanh grew up in a family that was not particularly religious. "They belonged to the Buddhist tradition," he said of his parents. "They practiced not a lot." Yet Nhat Hahn discovered his spiritual calling very early in life.

"In every one of us there is a baby monk or a baby nun. I was able to touch the baby monk in me when I was very little," Nhat Hanh said. "I was seven, and I saw a drawing of the Buddha sitting on the grass and looking very calm. Very, very calm. I said to myself, 'I want to be like that.' So the seed of the baby monk in me was watered."

"In every one of us there is a baby monk or a baby nun. I was able to touch the baby monk in me when I was very little," Nhat Hanh said. "I was seven, and I saw a drawing of the Buddha sitting on the grass and looking very calm. Very, very calm. I said to myself, 'I want to be like that.' So the seed of the baby monk in me was watered."

A little later, Nhat Hanh had an experience that convinced him of his destiny. He and his class went to the mountains for a picnic. "I was very excited because a hermit lived up there, and I had been told that a hermit is someone who practices to become a Buddha. But when we arrived on the mountain, very thirsty and very tired, I was very disappointed because the hermit wasn't there." Nhat Hanh guessed it was natural for a hermit to hide from a large group of people. So he set off to find the hermit on his own. "Suddenly, I heard the sound of water, like music." It was a natural well, where Nhat Hanh drank his fill, then slipped into a deep, restful sleep. "I had never had anything as delicious as that water, and it satisfied all my desires. I did not even want to see the hermit any more. In my little boy's brain I believed that the hermit had turned himself into the well so I could meet him privately."

As he grew up, Nhat Hanh witnessed the poverty and starvation of the Vietnamese people. The suffering around him reinforced his desire to enter reli-

Nhat Hanh said it took his parents a long time to accept their son's plans for a religious life. "My parents thought that monks have hard lives," he said. "But in fact, as a monk I have had a lot of happiness."

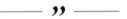

gious life. "It was a dream of a little boy to go out and learn Buddhism, to practice Buddhism in order to relieve the suffering of other people in society," he said. "Later on, when I became a novice monk, I also learned and practiced by this kind of desire." Nhat Hanh said it took his parents a long time to accept their son's plans for a religious life. "My parents thought that monks have hard lives, " he said. "But in fact, as a monk I have had a lot of happiness."

EDUCATION

When Nhat Hanh was a boy, Vietnamese education was guided by the French, who had colonized the country in 1884. "I attended elementary school, where French and Vietnamese were taught. We also learned a few hours of Chinese in elementary school," he said. "I had to learn history, geography, in French. And I also had to learn some Vietnamese history and geography in Vietnamese."

Nhat Hanh entered a Buddhist monastery at age 16 and completed his novitiate — or monk's training — at age 20. He studied literature and philosophy at Saigon University in Saigon, the major city in southern Vietnam. (It's now called Ho Chi Minh City.) Much later, in 1961, he traveled to the United States for graduate work in the philosophy of religion at Princeton University in New Jersey. During that period he also studied and taught Buddhism at Columbia University in New York City. Nhat Hanh is fluent in French and English as well as Vietnamese.

CAREER HIGHLIGHTS

Engaged Buddhism

During his early days as a monk, Nhat Hanh witnessed great suffering among the Vietnamese people. "There was a time when every morning when I got up I saw many dead bodies on the street because people did not have anything to eat," Nhat Hanh said. Students would go from house to house, begging for rice to give to the starving people. But they could not help everyone. "They were like God," he said of the students. "They had to decide who would live and who would die. I never can forget such an experience."

When Nhat Hanh was growing up in Vietnam, the country was a colony of France. After World War II ended in 1945, the country declared its independence. But France ruled over Vietnam until 1954, when Communist forces led by Ho Chi Minh took control of the north half of the country, which split the country into two separate nations: North Vietnam and South Vietnam. Communism is the name of a political and economic system based on the idea that all the people in a country should share equally in its property and resources. Communism eliminates most private property and gives it to the government to distribute as it sees fit. Under a Communist system, the central government exercises a great deal of control over the lives of citizens and places severe restrictions on individual rights. Throughout the 20th century, the United States was deeply opposed to the spread of Communism. The Soviet Union was a Communist country, as was China. A fierce rivalry developed between the U.S. and these nations, so when North Vietnam became Communist, it became an adversary of the United States. To prevent North Vietnam from conquering the South and to prevent the spread of Communism, the U.S. eventually gave military and economic aid to South Vietnam.

As the conflict between North and South Vietnam worsened, so did the suffering of the Vietnamese people. Nhat Hanh and his associates wanted to help the war's victims. They also wanted to promote non-violent resistance to the governments that started the war. But traditional Buddhism did not offer an outlet for these activities. So he and his colleagues founded what they called "engaged Buddhism." This practice combines traditional meditation with non-violent action to address social questions. Nhat Hanh says, "When I was in Vietnam, so many of our villages were being bombed. Along with my monastic brothers and sisters, I had to decide what to do. Should we continue to practice in our monasteries or should we leave the meditation halls in order to help the people who were suffering under the bombs? After careful reflection, we decided to do both — to go out and help people and to do so in mindfulness. We called it engaged Buddhism. Mindfulness must be engaged. Once there is seeing, there must be acting. Otherwise, what is the sense of seeing?" As he also said, "When bombs begin to fall on people, you cannot stay in the meditation hall all of the time."

In line with the teachings of engaged Buddhism, Nhat Hanh urged the Vietnamese people to demonstrate peacefully against the war. He suggested they protest by fasting, displaying religious altars in the streets to stop military tanks, refusing to cooperate with authorities, and shaving their heads. To help spread the message, Nhat Hanh established a publishing house and a weekly peace magazine. He founded Vietnam's first Buddhist high school and co-founded Van Hanh Buddhist University in Saigon.

> **"**
>
> *"When I was in Vietnam, so many of our villages were being bombed. Along with my monastic brothers and sisters, I had to decide what to do. Should we continue to practice in our monasteries or should we leave the meditation halls in order to help the people who were suffering under the bombs? After careful reflection, we decided to do both — to go out and help people and to do so in mindfulness. We called it engaged Buddhism. Mindfulness must be engaged. Once there is seeing, there must be acting. Otherwise, what is the sense of seeing?"*
>
> **"**

Another important aspect of engaged Buddhism was actively serving war's victims. Nhat Hanh helped to establish relief organizations for the injured and displaced. In 1963, he published *Engaged Buddhism,* an influential work that urged Buddhists to work for social change. In 1964, he founded the School of Youth Social Services. The SYSS, as it was called, drew about 10,000 student volunteers to its cause. The group rebuilt villages destroyed

Nhat Hanh's Way of Mindfulness

Nhat Hanh believes that people can become more conscious of society's needs by becoming "mindful" — that means living in intense awareness of each moment of life. He advocates slow, attentive breathing as the best way to be mindful. He explains: "You just become aware of the fact that you are breathing in — 'right now, I am breathing in — right now I am breathing out — I know that I am breathing out, and I enjoy my in-breath and I enjoy my out-breath.' Suddenly I am truly alive, truly present."

According to Nhat Hanh, this sense of presence can nurture inner peace. Inner peace, in turn, extends to the external world. So, in Nhat Hanh's teaching, the first step to peace on Earth is what he calls "being peace." (This is the title of one of his best-known books.) The inner peace leads to feelings of joy and gratitude. Ultimately, these emotions lead the individual to think of others less fortunate and to perform charitable acts.

Nhat Hanh and his followers use a bell to remind people to stop and practice a few calm, mindful breaths. He suggests that individuals should stop for three meditative breaths whenever they hear a bell — a church bell or even a telephone ringing. The bell, he said, "is the voice of the Buddha calling me to my true home."

Nhat Hanh suggests that mindfulness can be applied to any small act, such as walking, eating, or even washing the dishes. He advises followers to eat slowly and silently, taking time to chew every mouthful of food up to 50 times. He suggests that the eater then can contemplate where the food came from, how it was grown and prepared, and how it links the eater to the Earth, to other people, and to his or her own needs. As for dishwashing, he said: "If you take time to enjoy dishwashing, then dishwashing can become meditation. If you think of the time of washing as time that you lose, then you lose yourself. It means that you continue to lose your life."

Nhat Hanh urges people to engage — not run away from — the problems of the world. He discourages people from focusing on themselves. "When you focus on yourself, you find many more problems," he said. "Not realizing the suffering around you in the world — I don't think that is a happiness. You feel loneliness and emptiness, and these are more unbearable than other kinds of suffering. The most effective medicine is an experience of the suffering around you. Then you heal."

in the war. They provided schooling and medical care. They also worked toward reconciliation by refusing to support either side in the ongoing conflict, claiming that the enemies were not people but ideology, hatred, and ignorance. All the while, the meditative practices of traditional Buddhism remained at the forefront, as Nhat Hanh emphasized "mindfulness" (see sidebar on page 126). "You have to learn how to help a wounded child while still practicing mindful breathing. You should not allow yourself to get lost in action," Nhat Hanh said. "Action should be meditation at the same time."

Nhat Hanh the Peacemaker

It was during the first half of the 1960s that the United States began to give military support to the South Vietnamese government in its struggle against Communist North Vietnam. As the war escalated, Nhat Hanh received worldwide attention for his peace-making efforts. In 1966, as the guest of American peace activists, he visited the United States. Speaking for his people, he brought the message that the U.S. troops and bombs were more damaging to the Vietnamese people than their purported enemy, the North Vietnamese.

On his visit, Nhat Hanh met with top U.S. government officials, including Robert McNamara, the U.S. Defense Secretary. McNamara was an early

In his letter to the Nobel Prize Committee to nominate Thich Nhat Hanh for the Nobel Peace Prize, Dr. Martin Luther King wrote this:

"I do not personally know anybody more worthy of the Nobel Peace Prize than this gentle Buddhist monk from Vietnam," King wrote in his nominating letter. "I know Thich Nhat Hanh, and am privileged to call him my friend. Let me share with you some things I know about him. You will find in this single human being an awesome range of abilities and interests. He is a holy man, for he is humble and devout. He is a scholar of immense intellectual capacity. . . . [He] is also a poet of superb clarity and human compassion. . . . His ideas for peace, if applied, would build a monument to ecumenism, to world brotherhood, to humanity."

proponent of U.S. involvement in the Vietnam War. Nhat Hanh also won the support of Martin Luther King, Jr., the influential leader of the civil rights movement. With Nhat Hanh at his side, King spoke out publicly for the first time against American intervention in Vietnam. Many believe that King's declaration helped turn the tide of public opinion against U.S. involvement in the war. In 1964, King had been awarded the Nobel Peace Prize, the world's highest recognition for promoting peace and justice. In 1967, he nominated Nhat Hanh for the same honor. No winner was selected for the Peace Prize that year.

During his time in the United States, Nhat Hanh also befriended Thomas Merton, a Roman-Catholic monk and well-known spiritual author. Merton wrote this of Nhat Hanh: "He represents the young, the defenseless, the new ranks of youth who find themselves with every hand turned against them except those of the peasants and the poor, with whom they are working. Nhat Hanh speaks truly for the people of Vietnam." After leaving the United States, Nhat Hanh met with Pope Paul VI, leader of the worldwide Roman Catholic church, and gained his support in seeking peace.

Exiled from Vietnam

While he was away spreading his message of peace, Nhat Hanh received word that the South Vietnamese government had barred his return home. South Vietnamese officials believed that the Buddhists were their enemies. Nhat Hanh went to live in France, where he continued his work as energetically as ever. In 1967 he published *Vietnam: Lotus in a Sea of Fire*, his account of the destructiveness of the war. The book was influential and sold well in eight languages.

In 1969, Nhat Hanh headed the Vietnamese Buddhist Peace Delegation at a high-level conference in Paris aimed at ending the war. As a result of the talks, the United States eventually pulled out of Vietnam. Nhat Hanh and his colleagues in the delegation went to work to help Vietnamese refugees and orphans. Around the same time Nhat Hanh established the Unified Buddhist Church, a non-profit organization to represent him and his associates. In 1975, while he was in Paris, the North Vietnamese Communist government took over South Vietnam, reuniting the North and the South as one country, Vietnam. Its leaders also mistrusted Nhat Hanh and forbade him from returning home. From his exile in France, Nhat Hanh organized a large network to aid the Vietnamese people, including those who fled the country. Among the refugees he assisted were the "boat people," desperate refugees who risked their lives to escape Vietnam by sea on rickety boats.

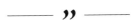

According to editor Arnold Kotler, "A monk since 1942, [Nhat Hanh] had taught several generations of novices in Vietnam, developing the skill of expressing the deepest teachings of Buddhism in straightforward yet poetic language. Because of his experience of war and his willingness to face the realities of our time, his teachings were very much about suffering, reconciliation, and peace."

Travels and Teachings

For five years, beginning in 1977, Nhat Hanh retreated to a small Buddhist community about a hundred miles southwest of Paris. In the early 1980s, he returned to the public eye. Nhat Hanh and his longtime associate, Sister Chan Khong, a Buddhist nun, co-founded Plum Village, a Buddhist community in southwest France. It is a retreat for spiritual pilgrims as well as a working plum orchard. All proceeds from the fruit go to needy children in Vietnam. About 100 nuns, monks, and lay people now live there. Thousands more come there each year to find spiritual guidance. Plum Village is part of a small network of monasteries and retreats now run by the Unified Buddhist Church, including sites in the United States, in Vermont and California.

Since his re-emergence, Nhat Hanh has traveled worldwide to lecture on engaged Buddhism and to lead retreats. In 1995, at a World Forum in San Francisco, he conducted a half-day session of walking meditation and mindful breathing for several world leaders, including the elder George Bush, former president of the United States; Margaret Thatcher, former prime minister of England; and Mikhail Gorbachev, former president of the Soviet Union. But more often, Nhat Hanh attracts ordinary people, often thousands at a time. He has held special retreats for such diverse groups as Vietnam veterans, psychotherapists, prison inmates, and ecologists. In the late 1990s, U.S. and other officials worked to persuade the Vietnamese government to lift Hanh's exile. But efforts failed when the Vietnamese officials insisted that only a government-sanctioned Buddhist organization could sponsor the visit. Nhat Hanh refused to accept the restriction.

> *According to Rev. Michael A. Fox, what Nhat Hanh does in his talks and writings "is to infuse the notion of inner peace with concrete meaning, bringing it down to earth in engaging, anecdotal, almost conversational language. By means of this endeavor, he clarifies the sense in which it can meaningfully be said that peace is already here, within us, or that peace begins with me. He delivers his message with skill, grace, and creative insight."*

His Writings

Nhat Hanh has also spread his teachings through his writings. He has written several types of works: poetry, essays on the practice of meditation, meditation exercises, and teachings on Buddhism. These are published by Parallax Press in Berkeley, California, which the church established to distribute his writings and tapes of his talks. Nhat Hanh has proven especially adept at teaching his beliefs. According to editor Arnold Kotler, "A monk since 1942, he had taught several generations of novices in Vietnam, developing the skill of expressing the deepest teachings of Buddhism in straightforward yet poetic language. Because of his experience of war and his willingness to face the realities of our time, his teachings were very much about suffering, reconciliation, and peace."

What Nhat Hanh does in his talks and writings, according to Rev. Michael A. Fox, "is to infuse the notion of inner peace with concrete meaning, bring-

ing it down to earth in engaging, anecdotal, almost conversational language. By means of this endeavor, he clarifies the sense in which it can meaningfully be said that peace is already here, within us, or that peace begins with me. He delivers his message with skill, grace, and creative insight."

Among Nhat Hanh's most popular works are *The Miracle of Mindfulness* (1987) and *Being Peace* (1987). Originally written in 1974 as a long letter to a fellow monk at the School of Youth Social Services, *The Miracle of Mindfulness* is a clear and simple guide to meditation. It includes anecdotes and exercises that can be used by any reader in the quest for self-understanding and peacefulness. It shows how mindfulness can be applied to each moment of the day, from washing dishes to answering the phone. *Being Peace* is an introduction to mindful living and engaged Buddhism. Now considered a classic, it shows how the pressures and demands of daily life can be transformed into the opportunity for peace. Both have sold hundreds of thousands of copies around the world.

In other works, including *Living Buddha, Living Christ* (1995), Nhat Hanh has focused on the common ground shared by followers of Christ and Buddha, two of the most pivotal figures in history. Nhat Hanh doesn't suggest that followers of other religions change their beliefs. In fact, he ex-

presses deep respect for Christian and Jewish traditions. But he does encourage people to discover their own religious roots by practicing Buddhist mindfulness. "It's not my intention to convert Christians or Jews into Buddhists," he said. "It's my intention to make them better Christians and better Jews." He believes that there are not serious divisions between Christianity and Buddhism. "Most of the boundaries we have created between our two traditions are artificial. Truth has no boundaries." Nhat Hanh often notes that in his room in Plum Village, his private altar holds images of Christ as well as Buddha. He lights incense in tribute to both.

In 2001 Nhat Hanh published *Anger: Wisdom for Cooling the Flames* (2001), his teachings on the peaceful resolution of conflict. The book was published just one day before the September 11, 2001, terrorist attacks on New York City and Washington, D.C. After that dreadful day, as Americans struggled to cope with their rage and fear in the wake of the attacks, many turned to Nhat Hanh's book for guidance.

In *Anger*, Nhat Hanh shows how anger can ruin people's lives and then shows how to change. He describes two techniques to promote communication and foster peace. First, he encourages compassionate listening, listening with full attention and compassion, but without judgment or criticism. Second, he recommends gentle and loving speech, which he describes as "the kind of language that conveys what is in our hearts, without blaming or condemning." As he explains, "We live in a time of many sophisticated means of communication. . . . But it is exactly at this time that communication between people, father and son, husband and wife, mother and daughter, has become extremely difficult. If we cannot restore communication, happiness will never be possible. In the Buddhist teaching, the practice of compassionate listening, the practice of loving speech, the practice of taking care of our anger, are presented very clearly. We have to put into practice the teaching of the Buddha . . . in order to restore communication and bring happiness to our family, our school, and our community. Then we can help other people in the world." Nhat Hanh emphasizes that these techniques can work for individuals and also for governments. As a reviewer wrote for *Publishers Weekly*, "Nhat Hanh doesn't limit his task to discussing anger between families and friends; he also deals with anger between citizens and governments." He has shared his practices with small groups of Palestinians and Israelis, who come to Plum Village hoping to find common ground in their bitter political struggles. Forty years after the height of the Vietnam War, his anti-war message is still strong. "It's plain that bombs have not removed terrorism, but only created more hatred and violence," Nhat Hanh said. "America is capable of compassion, understanding, and deep listening to the suffering of her people. These are the practices all of us must take up right away."

According to many commentators, Nhat Hanh has become the second most prominent spokesman for Buddhism in the non-Asian world. (The first is the Dalai Lama, the exiled religious leader of Tibet. More information on the Dalai Lama is available in *Biography Today*, Sep. 1998). Nhat Hanh has expressed his surprise at his influential role. "It was not my intention to come here to the West and spread Buddhism. The intention was to come here and try to end the Vietnam War. But because of that and because of the need of the people, our friends, that is why we had to begin to share the [Buddhist] practice with our Western friends."

As Nhat Hanh approaches age 80, his commitment to peace and tolerance remains strong. This is clear in his most recent book, *Creating True Peace: Ending Violence in Yourself, Your Family, Your Community, and the World* (2003), a blueprint for both personal change and global change. It acknowledges the current crisis of violence and people's feelings of helplessness and fear — while showing unequivocally that we are not helpless and that we can make a difference. Relying on Nhat Hahn's stories of his own experiences practicing peace during wartime, *Creating True Peace* includes meditation instruction and peace practices to show people how to create nonviolent thoughts even in the midst of upheaval. And it shows how to create peace throughout all aspects of life — personal, family, community,

"True peace is always possible. Yet it requires strength and practice, particularly in times of great difficulty. To some, peace and nonviolence are synonymous with passivity and weakness. In truth, practicing peace and nonviolence is far from passive. To practice peace, to make peace alive in us, is to actively cultivate understanding, love, and compassion, even in the face of misperception and conflict. Practicing peace, especially in times of war, requires courage."

state, nation, and world. "True peace is always possible. Yet it requires strength and practice, particularly in times of great difficulty. To some, peace and nonviolence are synonymous with passivity and weakness. In truth, practicing peace and nonviolence is far from passive. To practice peace, to make peace alive in us, is to actively cultivate understanding, love, and compassion, even in the face of misperception and conflict. Practicing peace, especially in times of war, requires courage."

HOME AND FAMILY

When he is not traveling, Nhat Hanh lives in Plum Village, a retreat consisting of old stone farmhouses in rural southwest France. He has never married or had children. But that doesn't mean he was denied a family. As he told the *San Francisco Chronicle*: "When I became a novice monk, I lived in a temple where the atmosphere was quite like in a family. The abbot is like a father and the other monks are like your big brothers, your small, younger brothers. It is a kind of a family. So I don't think that the desire to set up a family, to live like everyone else, was so strong, because it is clear that I had a happy time of being a novice. I had a lot of joy, of happiness." Although Nhat Hanh has not set foot in his homeland in more than 35 years, he is at peace with his situation. "In the beginning, I missed my country very much. I used to dream of going back," he said. "But now I feel that I am home."

HOBBIES AND INTERESTS

Nhat Hanh enjoys gardening. He is involved with tending the plum orchards in the Plum Village retreat in France.

SELECTED WRITINGS

Vietnam: Lotus in a Sea of Fire, 1967
Vietnam Poems, 1972
A Rose for Your Pocket, 1987
The Miracle of Mindfulness: A Manual on Meditation, 1987
Being Peace, 1987
The Moon Bamboo, 1989
Our Appointment with Life: The Buddha's Teaching on Living in the Present,
   1990
Old Path, White Clouds: Walking in the Footsteps of the Buddha, 1990

A Taste of Earth, and Other Legends of Vietnam, 1991
Touching Peace: Practicing the Art of Mindful Living, 1992
*The Blooming of a Lotus: Guided Meditation Exercises for Healing and
    Transformation,* 1993
Call Me by My True Name: The Collected Poems of Thich Nhat Hanh, 1993
Living Buddha, Living Christ, 1995
Be Still and Know: Reflections from Living Buddha, Living Christ, 1996
The Heart of a Buddha's Teaching: An Introduction to Buddhism, 1996
Teachings on Love, 1997
Interbeing: Fourteen Teachings for Engaged Buddhism, 1998
Fragrant Palm Leaves: Journals 1962-66, 1998
Going Home: Jesus and Buddha as Brothers, 2000
Anger: Wisdom for Cooling the Flames, 2001
Essential Writings, 2001
*Creating True Peace: Ending Violence in Yourself, Your Family, Your Community,
    and the World,* 2003

FURTHER READING

Books

Button, John. *The Radicalism Handbook: Radical Activists, Groups, and
    Movements of the Twentieth Century,* 1995
Contemporary Authors, Vol. 167
Powers, Roger, and William B. Vogele. *Protest, Power, and Change: An
    Encyclopedia of Nonviolent Action from Act-Up to Women's Suffrage,* 1997
Willis, Jennifer Schwamm, ed. *A Lifetime of Peace: Essential Writings by and
    about Thich Nhat Hanh,* 2003

Periodicals

Boston Globe, May 18, 2001, p.B1
Christian Century, Oct. 16, 1996, p.964
Christian Science Monitor, Apr. 4, 2002, p.18
Denver Post, Sep. 1, 2002, p.L6
Los Angeles Times, Sep. 11, 1999, p.2
National Catholic Reporter, July 16, 1993, p.11
New Yorker, June 25, 1966, p.21
New York Times, Sep. 19, 1993, p.A30; Oct. 16, 1999, p.A8
Peace Research, Aug. 2000, p.40
San Francisco Chronicle, Oct. 12 1997, p.3/Z1
Washington Post, Sep. 28, 1993, p.C1

Online Databases

Biography Resource Center Online, 2003, articles from *Contemporary Authors Online*, 2003, and *Contemporary Heroes and Heroines, Book IV*, 2000

ADDRESS

Thich Nhat Hanh
Maple Forest Monastery
P.O. Box 354
South Woodstock, VT 05071

WORLD WIDE WEB SITE

http://www.plumvillage.org

Keanu Reeves 1964-

Canadian Actor
Star of *Bill and Ted's Excellent Adventure, Speed,* and
The Matrix Trilogy

BIRTH

Keanu Charles Reeves was born on September 2, 1964, in
Beirut, Lebanon. Beirut is the capital of Lebanon, a country located on the Mediterranean Sea in the region known as the
Middle East. Keanu is the son of Samuel Nowlin Reeves, Jr., a
geologist, and Patricia Reeves, a stage performer from England
who later became a costume designer. His father, who is half-

Chinese and half-Hawaiian, gave him the name Keanu (pronounced key-AH-new), which is a Hawaiian word that means "cool breeze over the mountains." Keanu has a sister, Kim, who is two years younger, and a half-sister, Karina, who is 12 years younger, from his mother's later marriage to rock promoter Robert Miller.

YOUTH

Reeves's parents met in Beirut in the early 1960s, when he was working for an oil company and she was performing as a nightclub showgirl. Back then, the city was known as the "Paris of the Middle East." It was full of expensive hotels and casinos that served as popular vacation spots for wealthy Europeans. As their relationship deepened, both of his parents became heavily involved in the use of illegal drugs. His mother gave up drugs when they started a family, but his father refused to do so. As a result, Keanu's parents divorced when he was two years old.

By this time, the entire Middle East was engulfed in political turmoil and tensions between the Jewish state of Israel and the region's many Arab nations. In 1967 Patricia Reeves decided to leave Lebanon, believing that the escalating tensions between Israel and the region's Arab countries were building toward war. She took Keanu and his younger sister Kim to Australia,

Thanks to his mother's career as a costume designer, Reeves met a number of movie stars and musicians during his childhood. "I remember [rock star Alice Cooper] brought fake vomit and dog poo to terrorize the housekeeper," he recalled. *"He'd hang out, a regular dude. . . . I wrestled with him once."*

where they lived for a year, and then to New York City. In 1970 Patricia Reeves married a film and stage director named Paul Aaron. The family then relocated to Toronto, Canada, where Keanu spent the remainder of his childhood. Keanu grew close to his stepfather, who first sparked his interest in show business. His mother and Aaron divorced after a few years, but Keanu stayed in touch with his stepfather afterward and sometimes visited him during school breaks. During these visits Reeves often accompanied Aaron to work. He saw him direct such films as *A Force of One* and the television drama *The Miracle Worker*. This early exposure to filmmaking had an enormous impact on Reeves, who became a serious film buff. Before long, he was watching all sorts of movies, and he almost never missed the premiere of a new film at Toronto University's Repertory Cinema.

In the meantime, Patricia Reeves used her background in theatrical design to build a successful career as a costume designer. Over time, she created costumes for such stars as Dolly Parton and David Bowie. Thanks to his mother's career, Keanu met a number of movie stars and musicians during his childhood. "I remember [rock star Alice Cooper] brought fake vomit and dog poo to terrorize the housekeeper," he recalled. "He'd hang out, a regular dude. . . . I wrestled with him once." Meeting famous entertainers further increased Reeves's fascination with show business.

———— **"** ————

"You won't find any stories of poverty or ghettos in this dude's closet," Reeves once said. "When I see stuff in Los Angeles now, I realize how safe and sheltered my upbringing was. [Toronto] was a great place, no graffiti, cool people. The roughest it got was when we slung chestnuts at each other and built go-karts. I was a middle-class white boy with an absent father, a strong-willed mother, and two beautiful younger sisters."

———— **"** ————

In the mid-1970s Patricia Reeves married her third husband, rock promoter Robert Miller. This marriage lasted five years before ending in divorce. Keanu, meanwhile, continued to pay occasional visits to his biological father, who had settled in Hawaii. But Samuel Reeves abruptly disappeared when Keanu was 13 years old. Family members spent the next several years looking for him, but his whereabouts remained a mystery. Finally, in 1994 — the same year he starred in the blockbuster movie *Speed* — Keanu learned that his father had been arrested for dealing drugs. This news infuriated Reeves, who felt that it marked another instance in which his father had abandoned his family.

Although Reeves lived in four countries and had three different father figures during his childhood, he considered himself a normal kid. Growing up in Toronto, he had a paper route and a pet dog named Jupiter. He loved to eat peanut butter and crackers. He played ice hockey, and his skills as goalie earned him the nickname "The Wall." In addition, the success of his mother's business meant that the family was financially comfortable. "You won't find any stories of poverty or ghettos in this dude's closet," Reeves once said. "When I see stuff in Los Angeles now, I realize how safe and sheltered my upbringing was. [Toronto] was a great place, no graffiti, cool people. The roughest it got was when we slung chestnuts at each other and built go-karts. I was a middle-class white boy with an absent father, a strong-willed mother, and two beautiful younger sisters."

Still, Reeves did carry some emotional scars from his childhood. His father's disappearance left him feeling abandoned and empty. During his adolescence, he became something of a loner who had trouble forming close relationships with other people. "I think a lot of who I am is a reaction against [my father's] actions," he once said.

EDUCATION

Reeves was a poor student throughout his school years. His teachers at Jesse Ketchum Grade School in Toronto remember him as a kid who was always late for class and usually forgot his homework. Some of his problems in school stemmed from the fact that he suffered from dyslexia. Dyslexia is a condition in which the brain mixes up letters and numbers, making it very difficult to read. Reeves underwent special training that helped him overcome his dyslexia, but he still struggled with his schoolwork.

Reeves attended several different high schools in Toronto. He completed the ninth and tenth grades at North Toronto Collegiate School. He played on the basketball team and even joined the chess club. But he disliked the school's emphasis on structured learning, so he transferred to De La Salle College, a private Catholic high school. This move turned out to be a disaster for Reeves. He failed all of his courses except for Latin, which was the one subject that interested him. He even failed gym, even though he was an excellent athlete.

After one year at De La Salle, Reeves transferred to the Toronto School for the Performing Arts. Given his growing interest in acting, this should have been the perfect place for him. However, he was kicked out of the school in 1983 following an argument with his acting coach. At this point, Reeves dropped out of high school without earning a diploma. Instead, he enrolled in acting classes at the Leah Posluns Theatre School, which was located at a theater in a Toronto suburb. He studied formal acting techniques at the school, including proper breathing and how to "project" himself into a character.

FIRST JOBS

Reeves took his first tentative steps into the world of acting at age 14, when he began appearing in high school theatrical productions. "I started doing some acting and I got hooked—it allowed me to be somebody different," he explained. "I did a lot of pretending as a child. It was my way of coping." Nevertheless, he claimed that he did not decide to become an actor until he turned 18 and entered the Leah Posluns Theatre School. "I started taking classes at night, mostly out of respect for acting," he recalled. "I was taking classes and playing hockey a lot, and I started crashing some auditions with friends from the Performing Arts High School. I got some jobs, then I got an agent, and it all sort of fell together. I started doing community theater and commercials. I did a Coke commercial and this killer Kellogg's commercial."

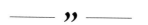

"I started doing some acting and I got hooked — it allowed me to be somebody different," Reeves explained. "I did a lot of pretending as a child. It was my way of coping."

Reeves built on this foundation to claim larger acting roles in Canadian television and theater. He was awarded a small part on the Canadian television show "Hangin' In," and he earned a starring role in the play *Wolfboy* at Toronto's Passe Muraille Theater. In *Wolfboy*, Reeves's character is placed in a mental hospital, where he meets a man who believes he is a werewolf. The play aroused some controversy for its homosexual themes, and Reeves's performance was panned by some critics. Even the director of the play, John Palmer, recognized that the young actor had problems. "He would skip words and say lines like he was trying to figure out what they meant," Palmer remembered. Like other actors, Reeves disliked hearing negative remarks about his performances. But he did not let the comments distract him from his goal of building a successful acting career.

As a young adult, Reeves also developed a passion for the plays of William Shakespeare. He read all of the great playwright's works and memorized many of the lines. His knowledge of Shakespeare helped him win the role of Mercutio in *Romeo and Juliet* at the Hedgerow Theater in Pennsylvania. Armed with this experience, Reeves auditioned for the prestigious Shakespeare Festival in Stratford, Ontario. When he failed to win any roles, he decided to move to Los Angeles and try to break into American movies.

CAREER HIGHLIGHTS

Keanu Reeves is a hard-working, prolific actor who has appeared in over 40 films. He has worked in a wide range of genres, from comedy to horror

Reeves and Ione Skye Leitch (Clarissa) co-starred in the controversial film
River's Edge.

and from romance to action films. He has appeared in small, independent films as well as big-budget blockbusters. Throughout his career, Reeves has been criticized by reviewers who claim that he has a bland, emotionless style of acting. In fact, some critics have dubbed him the worst actor in Hollywood. But Reeves has overcome this label to become one of the world's most popular and highest-paid movie stars. He has starred in some of the most successful movies of the past two decades, including *Bill and Ted's Excellent Adventure, Speed, The Matrix, The Matrix Reloaded,* and *The Matrix Revolutions.*

Getting Started

In 1986, at the age of 21, Reeves drove his 1969 Volvo to Los Angeles. He moved in with his former stepfather, director Paul Aaron, who helped him find an agent. Within a few weeks, Reeves landed a supporting role as a hockey goalie in the 1986 movie *Youngblood,* which also featured Rob Lowe and Patrick Swayze. Other parts quickly followed. For example, in 1986 he also worked with Charles Bronson in the movie *Act of Vengeance,* appeared in a film about alcoholism called *Under the Influence,* and sang in the television musical *Babes in Toyland.*

143

Reeves's big break came that same year, when he won a supporting role in the disturbing and thought-provoking teen drama *River's Edge* (1986). The plot is based on a true story about a teenager who kills his girlfriend and leaves her body next to a river. The movie traces what happens when the boy tells his rebellious group of friends about his crime. All of the teens come from poor homes and lack parental supervision and moral guidance. Their feelings of alienation and hopelessness allow them to disregard the murder, and they all agree not to tell their parents or the police. But a few days later, one of the killer's friends, Matt (played by Reeves), breaks down under feelings of guilt and reports the crime. *River's Edge* received positive reviews from critics, although it did not fare particularly well at the box office. Several critics praised Reeves's performance. In a review for *Time* magazine, for example, Richard Schickel said he played the part of Matt with "exemplary restraint," and *People* magazine reviewer Peter Tranvis called his performance "sharply characterized."

Although Reeves was not yet a star, he worked consistently over the next few years. His work included a couple of successful films as well as a number of stinkers. One of his films that earned good reviews was *Dangerous Liaisons* (1988), a period drama set in 18th-century France. His co-stars included Glenn Close, Michelle Pfeiffer, John Malkovich, and Uma Thurman. The following year Reeves appeared alongside Steve Martin, Mary Steenburgen, and Dianne Wiest in *Parenthood* (1989), a popular comedy about the struggles involved in family life, shown through multiple generations in a large extended family. He played the weird but good-hearted boyfriend of one of the family members in the film.

Bill and Ted's Excellent Adventure

Reeves gained his first taste of fame with the 1989 release of the teen comedy *Bill and Ted's Excellent Adventure*. This silly time-travel adventure starred Reeves as the dim-witted Ted Logan and Alex Winter as the equally dense Bill Preston. Bill and Ted are terrible musicians who form a band called the Wyld Stallyns. They dream of becoming rock stars, but their dream is threatened by their poor grades in high school. If Ted fails history, his father will send him away to military school and break up the band.

As the boys agonize over this possibility, a telephone booth falls out of the sky. Inside is a man named Rufus (played by George Carlin) who says he is from the future. Rufus has traveled through time to help the boys in the present, because it turns out that the Wyld Stallyns eventually become famous and influence the world of the future. Rufus claims that the peaceful world of the future may not exist if the boys fail their history final exam.

The success of Bill and Ted's Excellent Adventure *brought Reeves movie stardom.*

Bill and Ted use the phone booth as a time machine to travel to various eras in history and meet famous figures of the past. They learn about history firsthand through a series of crazy adventures. In the end, the teens

145

transport Abraham Lincoln, Socrates, Beethoven, Joan of Arc, Genghis Khan, and other historical figures back to their school to stage a wild show for their oral history exam. *Bill and Ted's Excellent Adventure* won the approval of young audiences and became a surprise box-office hit. The low-budget picture, which was filmed for about $10 million, ended up grossing over $45 million in theaters.

Reeves enjoyed his role in the film. "I got to play a guy who's like a child of nature," he said of Ted. "He's almost an idiot savant, except he's not that smart. But he's pure and good. He's a good soul." Reeves returned to the role in the 1991 sequel *Bill and Ted's Bogus Journey*, in which the boys travel to heaven and hell. Upon meeting God, Ted says in his typical goofy fashion, "Congratulations on a most excellent planet. Bill and I enjoy it on a daily basis." The boys later play the devil in a game of Battleship in order to save their souls.

——— **"** ———

"I got to play a guy who's like a child of nature," Reeves said of the character Ted. "He's almost an idiot savant, except he's not that smart. But he's pure and good. He's a good soul."

——— **"** ———

While the success of the *Bill and Ted* movies brought Reeves stardom, it also contributed to a lasting image of him as a limited and rather vapid actor who could only play teen roles. Reeves admitted that he sometimes fostered this image by using Ted's "Valleyspeak" language in interviews. "Ted hung a label on me," he confessed, "and I hung a label on myself, to a certain extent."

Expanding His Range as an Actor

After the *Bill and Ted* films, Reeves took on a variety of challenging roles in an effort to avoid being typecast. For example, he returned to his love of Shakespeare by doing a summer workshop production of *The Tempest* in Massachusetts. He also co-starred with Patrick Swayze in the 1991 action-thriller *Point Break*. In this film, which was a box office success despite mediocre reviews, Reeves plays an undercover FBI agent who takes up surfing in order to infiltrate a group of criminals.

Also in 1991, Reeves starred in the controversial movie *My Own Private Idaho* with River Phoenix, a long-time friend (for more information, see *Biography Today*, Apr. 1994). Both actors appeared in the film in hopes of escaping their teen-idol images and branching out into more challenging material. In this film, Reeves plays Scott Favor, a lazy, Shakespeare-quoting

Reeves as Jonathan Harker is confronted with Dracula (Gary Oldman).

rich kid who is waiting to turn 21 so he can inherit his father's fortune. In the meantime, he becomes involved in the underground world of homosexual street hustlers. He makes friends with Mike Waters (Phoenix), a fellow hustler who suffers from narcolepsy (a condition in which people fall asleep without warning). Scott helps Mike search for his missing mother, but all the while he plans to return to his rich family once he receives his inheritance.

My Own Private Idaho was controversial because of its homosexual themes, violence, and gritty depiction of the life of male prostitutes. In order to prepare for their roles, Reeves and Phoenix hung out with real-life street hustlers and experimented with drugs. Reeves was able to put the drug use behind him, but Phoenix developed an addiction. In 1993, Phoenix died of a drug overdose outside a Los Angeles nightclub. Reeves was devastated by the death of his friend.

In 1992 Reeves appeared in *Bram Stoker's Dracula,* a retelling of the famous vampire legend. In a cast that included Anthony Hopkins, Winona Ryder, and Gary Oldman, he played London lawyer Jonathan Hacker. Hacker goes to Dracula's castle to discuss a real estate matter, but he finds much more than he bargained for when he meets the vampire and his bloodsucking brides.

Although *Bram Stoker's Dracula* did fairly well in theaters, Reeves's performance generated some of the harshest criticism of his career. One critic quipped, "[Reeves] is so limited and stamped with his *Bill and Ted* roles you can practically hear him saying, 'Most excellent fangs, Drac dude.'" The actor himself admitted he was not very good in the movie, partly because he found it difficult to master an English accent. "I got killed in *Dracula*—I got slaughtered," he acknowledged. "The other actors' performances were so operatic, and I didn't hold up my end of the bargain. My performance was too introverted, closed in, and safe. Since *Dracula* came out I've always felt that I could have played it much more aggressive. . . . I didn't act very well. I'll leave it at that."

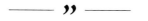

Speed *was a huge hit at the box office and established Reeves as a new breed of sensitive action hero.* "At last an action picture out of Hollywood that satisfies," *wrote John Simon in* National Review.

Reeves chose yet another unusual role in 1993, when he played Prince Siddhartha in the film *Little Buddha*. The main story concerns a young American boy who is believed to be the reincarnation of an important lama, or Buddhist holy man. Buddhist monks from the Asian country of Tibet come to Seattle to meet the boy and convince his parents to let him visit their monastery in the Himalayas. A series of flashbacks to ancient India shows the transformation of Siddhartha from a spoiled young prince into the serene spiritual leader known as Buddha. *Little Buddha* received mixed reviews, as did Reeves's performance. Some critics felt that he was miscast, but others claimed that his low-key acting style worked well in the role. Stanley Kauffmann of the *New Republic*, for example, said Reeves played Siddhartha with "surprising grace and focus."

Becoming an Action Hero in *Speed*

Reeves's popularity soared to new heights when he starred in the 1994 action-blockbuster *Speed*. He played Jack Traven, a heroic police officer who matches wits with a deranged ex-cop looking for revenge (played by Dennis Hopper). The main action of the film takes place on a speeding bus that contains a bomb set to explode if the bus slows down below 50 miles per hour. With the help of Annie (played by Sandra Bullock), an attractive young woman who takes the wheel when the bus driver is injured, Traven saves the passengers and confronts the madman. *Speed* was a huge hit at the box office and established Reeves as a new breed of sensitive action hero. "At last an action picture out of Hollywood that satisfies," wrote John Simon in *National Review*.

Thanks to the success of *Speed*, Reeves's asking price per picture increased to $7 million. Yet he turned down an amazing $11 million to reprise his role as Jack Traven in the sequel *Speed 2*. Reeves did not like the script and was not eager to be pigeon-holed as an action hero. Instead, he chose to play the title role in *Hamlet* for $2,000 per week at a small theater in Winnipeg, Canada. "To perform Shakespeare you get to say very profound words and in the body it feels more thrilling," he explained. "Your spirit, your intellect, your heart, and your voice all have to, at a very high degree, melt into the speaking of words and behavior. For me all of these things are missing in action pictures. In Shakespeare, it's pure." For the first few performances, Reeves was noticeably nervous playing the challenging character of Hamlet. But he eventually grew into the role. In fact, Roger Lewis of *Vanity Fair* called him "one of the top three Hamlets I have seen."

Reeves's next starring role came in the 1995 futuristic action movie *Johnny Mnemonic*. He plays the title character, who has the ability to store computer data inside his brain. He works as a high-tech courier, delivering sensitive information in person to prevent it from being intercepted by computer hackers. But he is forced to run for his life when a group of criminals seeks to capture him and seize the data he is carrying. Unfortunately, *Johnny Mnemonic* was a box office disappointment, and critics lined up to deliver scathing reviews of the film. In *Entertainment Weekly*, for example, reviewer Owen Gleiberman wrote that "*Johnny Mnemonic*, a slack and derivative future-shock thriller, offers the embarrassing spectacle of Keanu Reeves working overtime to convince you that he has too much on his mind."

In 1997 Reeves starred opposite Al Pacino in the supernatural thriller *The Devil's Advocate*. Reeves plays Kevin Lomax, a successful Florida criminal-

defense attorney who joins a powerful, glitzy New York law firm. Eager to please his new boss, John Milton (Pacino), Kevin grows increasingly immoral and ruthless. But his relationship with his wife, Mary Ann (Charlize Theron), begins to fall apart. Eventually, however, Kevin begins to understand his boss's intentions, triggering a dramatic showdown. Although the film received generally poor reviews, some critics admitted that it kept their interest. "*The Devil's Advocate* is a fairly entertaining supernatural potboiler that finally bubbles over with a nearly operatic sense of absurdity and excess," Todd McCarthy wrote in *Variety*. "Reeves does a serious and pleasing job in believably conveying Kevin's legal skill, personal allure, and willingness to be distracted from domestic life by the heady experience of big-city success."

The Matrix

For five years following the release of *Speed*, none of Reeves's films achieved more than mild success. But this situation changed dramatically in 1999, when Reeves starred in an action-packed science-fiction film called *The Matrix*. In this film, Reeves plays Thomas Anderson, a 21st-century computer programmer who secretly acts as a hacker under the nickname Neo. Late one night, Neo is awakened from his ordinary life to discover that the world is not as it seems.

"I'd be a liar if I told you I understood everything that was going on when I first read the script,"Reeves said about **The Matrix.** *"But I knew immediately that I had never read anything like it and that I wanted to be part of it. I had no idea it would become what it has become. . . . I was just happy to be part of something that was so original and challenging."*

Under the guidance of the mysterious Morpheus (Lawrence Fishburne), Neo learns that a race of intelligent machines has taken over Earth. The machines control human beings and use their bodies as a source of energy. In order to keep the human race dormant, the machines use a sophisticated computer simulation to convince people that they remain free and are living a normal life. What millions of people perceive as reality is in fact an elaborate, computer-generated hallucination—a type of virtual reality. Only a few people have escaped the control of the machines. Led by Morpheus, they have formed bands of underground freedom fighters to try to regain control of the planet.

As Neo struggles to understand and accept this awful truth, he receives another shock. Morpheus believes that Neo is "the One," a great hero who is destined to help the humans overcome the oppressive machines. With the help of Morpheus, another freedom fighter named Trinity (Carrie-Anne Moss), and others, Neo works hard to develop his intellectual powers and fighting abilities in order to fulfill his destiny.

Reeves was determined to win the role of Neo from the first time he read the movie script. The scripts for *The Matrix* and its sequels were written by Andy and Larry Wachowski, who also directed the films. Reeves was intrigued by the complex, yet highly original story and characters. "I'd be a liar if I told you I understood everything that was going on when I first read the script," he noted. "But I knew immediately that I had never read anything like it and that I wanted to be part of it. I had no idea it would become what it has become. . . . I was just happy to be part of something that was so original and challenging."

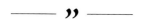

> "The Matrix *changed not only the way we look at movies, but movies themselves,"David Edelstein wrote in the* New York Times. *"The Matrix* cut us loose from the laws of physics in ways that no live-action film had ever done, exploding our ideas of time and space on screen."

Reeves underwent months of preparation before filming began. He jumped into a strenuous training routine to achieve top conditioning for the physically demanding role. He also studied martial arts so that he could perform most of his own stunts in the film's long fight sequences. "We knew it would take a maniacal commitment," director Larry Wachowski stated. "Keanu was our maniac." "Keanu was amazing," added producer Joel Silver. "He put his life and career on hold to learn to do the fights. Even after intense training and with all the precautions, the actors would hurt their wrists and ribs on a daily basis. Keanu never once complained or played the prima donna."(For more information on the film's martial arts choreography, see the entry on Yuen Wo-Ping in *Biography Today Performing Artists,*Vol. 3.)

The Matrix became a huge, unexpected hit within a few weeks of its release. It enjoyed tremendous word-of-mouth among moviegoers because it was so different from anything they had ever seen before. Writer-directors Andy and Larry Wachowski, known simply as "the brothers," ac-

A scene from The Matrix.

knowledged such influences as American comic books, Chinese kung fu pictures, Japanese anime, and world philosophy and spiritual texts. They used state-of-the art, computer-generated images and spectacular special effects to bring the story to life. Shot in Australia for $63 million, *The Matrix* grossed an incredible $460 million in worldwide box office receipts.

The popularity of *The Matrix* changed the look of action movies from that time forward. In fact, *Entertainment Weekly* called it "the most influential action movie of its generation." Since its release, countless other movies have featured 360-degree camera sweeps, bullets rippling through the air in slow motion, and heroes wearing black trench coats and trendy sunglasses. "*The Matrix* changed not only the way we look at movies, but movies themselves," David Edelstein wrote in the *New York Times*. "*The Matrix* cut us loose from the laws of physics in ways that no live-action film had ever done, exploding our ideas of time and space on screen." The phenomenal success of *The Matrix* soon spawned two sequels, *The Matrix Reloaded* and *The Matrix Revolutions*. But first, Reeves appeared in several very different films.

Looking for Variety in Recent Projects

After starring in *The Matrix*, Reeves looked for roles that were as different as possible from Neo. In 2000 he starred in *The Replacements,* a feel-good sports story about a group of misfit athletes who fill in when professional football players hold a labor strike against the National Football League (NFL). Reeves plays Shane Falco, a star college quarterback whose disastrous play in his last college bowl game cost him a chance at NFL stardom. He is making a living by scraping barnacles off the bottoms of rich people's

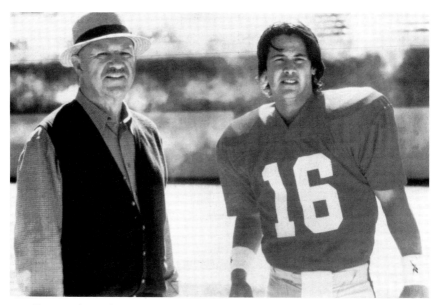

Reeves, shown here with Gene Hackman, gave a noteworthy performance in The Replacements.

yachts when he is recruited to help the fictional Washington Sentinels finish the season. Though most critics claimed that the movie followed a familiar formula, some praised Reeves's performance. "When it matters most, *The Replacements* really does engage you emotionally and make you root for this ragtag, madcap, zany pack of wackies," reviewer Tom Shales said on National Public Radio's *Morning Edition*. "A team depends on its quarterback, and so does this film. . . . He's winningly played by Keanu Reeves."

Reeves received glowing reviews for his supporting role in the 2000 thriller *The Gift*. This film follows the story of a psychic (Cate Blanchett) whose visions lead her to the heart of a murder mystery in a small Southern town. Reeves plays Donnie Barksdale, a mean-tempered redneck who beats his wife, Valerie (Hilary Swank), and stalks the psychic. Reeves spent several weeks hanging out with rough characters in the South to prepare for the role. His preparation seemed to pay off. The film received only fair reviews, but Reeves received a great deal of notice for his menacing performance. "Keanu Reeves is bad, very bad in *The Gift*. But intentionally, and quite effectively," wrote Bob Strauss in the *Guardian*.

In 2001 Reeves took a romantic leading role opposite Charlize Theron in *Sweet November*. Theron plays a free-spirited San Francisco woman who finds a new boyfriend every month. When she meets advertising executive Nelson Moss, played by Reeves, they become romantically involved for the month of November. The couple ends up falling in love, but it turns out that she is hiding a tragic secret. *Sweet November* received poor reviews and achieved only moderate success at the box office. "The movie is a very low-grade romantic drama indeed, a love story with all the life-and-death intensity of a heat rash," wrote Lisa Schwarzbaum in *Entertainment Weekly*.

Also in 2001, Reeves appeared in the family-oriented movie *Hardball*. He plays Conor O'Neill, a hard-drinking Irish gambler who repays a favor by taking over the coaching responsibilities for a hard-luck Little League baseball team. He experiences conflict with the members of the team, a group of underprivileged African-American kids from a local housing pro-

Reeves took a romantic leading role opposite Charlize Theron in the love story Sweet November.

ject. But the coach and the players ultimately bond together to make an exciting championship run. "*Hardball* works where it counts, on the emotional level," wrote Bob Graham in the *San Francisco Chronicle*. "Some of the movie's heart-tugging effects stack the deck — one is a whopper — but Reeves, as a borderline alcoholic and compulsive gambler, makes up for it with a very sympathetic performance."

"I've been working out for up to three hours a day and I reckon I'm in the greatest physical condition I've ever been in my life. I've been training with a mix of aerobics, weights, kick-boxing, and karate," Reeves noted. *"This is more physically demanding than the original movie. Trust me, you would not want to be my knees in the morning before I start limbering up."*

Returning as Neo in Two Highly Anticipated Sequels

By the time those movies were out in theaters, Reeves was already back at work on the sequels to *The Matrix*: *The Matrix Reloaded* and *The Matrix Revolutions*. The two sequels were filmed back-to-back, first in California for several months in mid-2000 and then in Australia from September 2001 through August 2002; they were released in May and November of 2003. Reeves received a record paycheck of $30 million for appearing in the two movies. He also received 15 percent of the gross box-office receipts, which was expected to increase the total to between $90 and $200 million. He thus became the best-paid actor in Hollywood in 2003.

In *The Matrix Reloaded*, Neo continues to battle against the non-human forces of the matrix. He is beginning to learn how to control his powers, as he remains locked in a massive struggle with Agent Smith. He is also beginning to understand the mysteries of the matrix. The machine world is out to destroy the underground city of Zion, where the few remaining free humans live. Neo and his friends must fight to protect Zion from the machines that control the rest of humanity, and time is running out. "The film picks up six months after the first movie ended with Neo having 72 hours to stop 250,000 probes from discovering mankind's last stronghold," Reeves explained. The film ended in a cliffhanger, leaving the audience wondering what would happen next.

The Wachowski brothers ramped up the action in the sequel and included a number of special effects never before seen on screen. "There are more

Scenes from The Matrix Reloaded.

action sequences than the last film, and instead of fighting one-to-one I fight one-against-many, although the writers have made the movie more sophisticated and demanding," Reeves stated. The best-known example of the film's unique effects is the Burly Brawl — an extended fight sequence between Neo and his main rival, Agent Smith (Hugo Weaving), in which Smith continually duplicates himself. Neo eventually ends up facing dozens of agents in the battle. The Burly Brawl features lots of computer-generated characters blended with footage of the actors performing their own stunts. Reeves trained for nine weeks to perfect the 500 moves he performs in the scene.

> ── " ──
>
> *Reeves claimed that he enjoyed the physical demands of* **The Matrix** *series. "I've always been a bit reckless," he admitted. "The more physical acting gets, the more comfortable I feel. I love the danger in doing stunts and physical stuff in films."*
>
> ── " ──

In *The Matrix Revolutions*, the concluding chapter of the series, the story focuses on the war between humans and machines. The story takes place inside the matrix, in Zion, and in Machine City. The movie opens with Neo trapped in limbo between the world of the matrix and the real world. He eventually escapes and meets Smith in battle once again. Meanwhile, the humans of Zion engage in a spectacular battle against the machines that want to destroy them. In addition, several pivotal scenes take place in Machine City, where Neo continues his quest to save humanity.

As he did in the first movie, Reeves trained hard in order to perform nearly all of his own stunts in *The Matrix Reloaded* and *The Matrix Revolutions*. "I've been working out for up to three hours a day and I reckon I'm in the greatest physical condition I've ever been in my life. I've been training with a mix of aerobics, weights, kick-boxing, and karate," he noted. "This is more physically demanding than the original movie. Trust me, you would not want to be my knees in the morning before I start limbering up." But Reeves claimed that he enjoyed the physical demands of *The Matrix* series. "I've always been a bit reckless," he admitted. "The more physical acting gets, the more comfortable I feel. I love the danger in doing stunts and physical stuff in films." Indeed, the action sequences were widely considered the most impressive parts of the new films.

Unfortunately, the final two installments of *The Matrix* series did not earn the acclaim enjoyed by the opening film. "The original *Matrix* was full of

Scenes from The Matrix Revolutions.

———— " ————

"I love Neo. I find Neo to be a beautiful man. I love his dignity, his love for Trinity, his search. Playing him is like playing the best parts of us. I like that he's a man who, in **The Matrix,** *has this superhuman ability but also has this incredible responsibility,"Reeves said. "I love* **The Matrix**—*love it through and through. And so the sacrifices—what it demands, what it hopes for—had me body and soul. And to feel that is one of the more remarkable things in my life."*

———— " ————

dizzying surprises," wrote *Newsweek* critic David Ansen. "But it's turned out that the Wachowskis didn't have many more tricks up their sleeves. . . . Though they're full of undeniably spectacular moments, great production values, and unusual ambition, a simple thing has gotten lost in these sequels: they're not much fun."

Many critics and fans expressed some disappointment with the final two films of *The Matrix* series, saying that they didn't live up to the incredible promise of the first film. But the movies did earn Reeves legions of new fans. "*The Matrix* series has seen [Reeves] reborn as the last word in cool machismo—and it's a role for which his lack of animation is ideally suited," wrote Christopher Tookey in the *Daily Telegraph*. "He is having the last laugh on all his critics." "The success or failure of a Reeves performance depends greatly on how well he's chosen—on whether the role flatters his uneven gifts," added Lucy Kaylin in *GQ* magazine. "No actor dead or alive has ever been better matched with a role than Reeves is with Neo, the computer hacker who comes to learn that humans are living in a sinister dreamscape generated by machines that are actually, systematically, turning them into batteries. . . . Apart from being a slick and credible action hero, he owned the movie because he committed so totally, fusing himself to its arcane internal logic. And his ramrod seriousness underscored the notion of profound questions lurking beneath the elaborate cinematic armature."

For his part, Reeves enjoyed playing the role of Neo, and he felt a twinge of sadness when filming of *The Matrix* series concluded. "I love Neo. I find Neo to be a beautiful man. I love his dignity, his love for Trinity, his search. Playing him is like playing the best parts of us. I like that he's a man who, in *The Matrix,* has this superhuman ability but also has this incredible responsibility," he said. "I love *The Matrix*—love it through and through. And so the sacrifices—what it demands, what it hopes for—had me body and soul. And to feel that is one of the more remarkable things in my life."

Recent Projects

After wrapping up the *Matrix* series, Reeves turned his attention to a role totally different from his Neo character. He played a doctor in *Something's Gotta Give* (2003), a romantic comedy with Jack Nicholson and Diane Keaton. When asked about his flair for playing wildly different personalities from film to film, he explained that "My goal remains the same [throughout my career]: to play different types of characters and do different kinds of films in style and scope. I guess it's just me wanting to act and not be just one thing."

HOME AND FAMILY

Although Reeves has been romantically linked to a number of women, he has never been married. "I'm a coward, frightened of falling in love. Isn't everybody?" he noted. "It would be great to marry because it would be very important to me to have a home and a family, but work means I'm on the road a lot and when I'm working I think only about work." Reeves's most serious relationship was with actress Jennifer Syme, who became pregnant with his child in 1999. Sadly, the baby girl was stillborn and the couple broke up a short time later. In 2001 the couple tried to reconcile, but Syme was killed in a tragic automobile accident.

Reeves remains close to his mother and his two younger sisters. He took time off from acting in the late 1990s to help his sister Kim battle leukemia (a type of cancer that affects the blood). "The last few years have been tough for me," he admitted.

Because his busy filming schedule kept him on the road for long periods of time, Reeves resisted buying a home of his own for many years. Instead, he lived in hotels or with friends. "I don't need a house," he said at the time. "I prefer to be free, unfettered. I like being in the desert or high in a tree. I'm not a homebody type of guy." But Reeves recently changed his mind. He bought a three-bedroom, 5,600-square-foot contemporary home in the Hollywood Hills, with glass walls that overlook the ocean and the Los Angeles skyline. Reeves has not lived in Canada for many years, but he maintains his Canadian citizenship, which dates back to his childhood in Toronto.

Reeves with his band, Dogstar, *in 2000.*

HOBBIES AND OTHER INTERESTS

In addition to acting, Reeves has two great passions: riding motorcycles and playing bass guitar. As a guitarist, he plays in the band Dogstar, which also includes singer Bret Domrose and drummer Rob Mailhouse. "I'm committed to it as long as we're interested in writing together and playing," he said of the band. "For me, it's a great experience when I'm not working, because there's kind of a carefree aspect to it that I cherish. It's a different kind of good time. I hope that my band brothers will keep enjoying it and get along. It's hard to keep a band together, but we're working on it." Some of Reeves's quieter hobbies include playing chess and reading.

SELECTED CREDITS

Films

Youngblood, 1986
River's Edge, 1986
Dangerous Liaisons, 1988
Parenthood, 1989
Bill and Ted's Excellent Adventure, 1989
Point Break, 1991
Bill and Ted's Bogus Journey, 1991

My Own Private Idaho, 1991
Bram Stoker's Dracula, 1992
Much Ado about Nothing, 1993
Little Buddha, 1993
Speed, 1994
Johnny Mnemonic, 1995
A Walk in the Clouds, 1995
Feeling Minnesota, 1996
The Devil's Advocate, 1997
The Matrix, 1999
The Replacements, 2000
The Gift, 2000
Sweet November, 2001
Hardball, 2001
The Matrix Reloaded, 2003
The Matrix Revolutions, 2003
Something's Gotta Give, 2003

Recordings

Happy Ending, 2000 (with Dogstar)

HONORS AND AWARDS

MTV Movie Award as Most Desirable Male: 1991, for *Point Break*
MTV Movie Award as Best On-Screen Duo: 1994, for *Speed* (with Sandra
  Bullock)

FURTHER READING

Books

Bystedt, Karen Hardy. *Before They Were Famous: In Their Own Words,* 1996
Goodrich, J.J. *The Keanu Matrix: Unraveling the Puzzle of Hollywood's
  Reluctant Superstar,* 2003
Membery, York. *Superstars of Film: Keanu Reeves,* 1998
Nickson, Chris. *Keanu Reeves,* 1996
Robb, Brian J. *Keanu Reeves,* 1997

Periodicals

Biography, Sep. 2000, p.52
Current Biography Yearbook, 1995

Entertainment Weekly, Oct. 29, 1993, p.12; June 10, 1994, p.20; July 21, 1995, p.61; June 14, 1996, p.7; Sep. 6, 1996, p.75; Apr. 9, 1999, p.26; Feb. 16, 2001, p.81; May 16, 2003, p.24; Nov. 7, 2003, p.24
GQ, May 2003, p.147
Maclean's, Jan. 23, 1995, p.52
New Republic, Dec. 14, 1992, p.28; July 4, 1994, p.26
New York Times, Dec. 19, 1986, p.C38; June 6, 1987, p.9; July 29, 1995, p.11; May 11, 2003, p.AR1; Nov. 5, 2003, p.E1
Newsweek, May 5, 2003, p.56; Nov. 10, 2003, p.63
People, Mar. 13, 1989, p.16; July 22, 1991, p.10; Sep. 30, 1991, p.18; Nov. 16, 1992, p.25; June 20, 1994, p.18; July 11, 1994, p.49; May 8, 1995, p.82; June 5, 1995, p.70; June 5, 2000, p.18; Aug. 28, 2000, p.17; June 2, 2003, p.63
Time, June 1, 1987, p.73; Oct. 28, 1991, p.101; Feb. 6, 1995, p.79; Apr. 5, 1999, p.68; Apr. 19, 1999, p.75; May 12, 2003, p.64
USA Today, June 9, 1994, p.D1; May 24, 1995, p.D2; Aug. 4, 2000, p.E1; Aug. 9, 2000, p.D6; Nov. 5, 2003, p.D5
Vanity Fair, Feb. 2001, p.108
Variety, Nov. 3, 2003, p.30
Washington Post, Jan. 19, 2001, p.T42

Online Databases

Biography Resource Center Online, 2003, article from *International Dictionary of Films and Filmmakers, Vol. 3: Actors and Actresses,* 1996

ADDRESS

Keanu Reeves
Creative Artists Agency
9830 Wilshire Blvd.
Beverly Hills, CA 90212

WORLD WIDE WEB SITES

http://whatisthematrix.warnerbrothers.com
http://www.biography.com
http://entertainment.msn.com/celebs
http://www.eonline.com

Alexa Vega 1988-
American Actress
Stars as Carmen Cortez in the Popular *Spy Kids*
Movie Trilogy

BIRTH

Alexa Vega was born on August 27, 1988, in Miami, Florida.
She is of Colombian and Italian ancestry and is fluent in Spanish. She has three younger sisters, Krizia, Makenzie (who also
acts), and Greylin, plus an older half-sister, Margaux. Her
mother, Gina Rue, was a model and actress who now serves as
Vega's manager. No information is available about her father.

—— " ——

Despite her success as an actress, Vega still faces the same types of experiences at school that all kids face. She had this to say about ninth grade: "To a certain extent it's wonderful but you still have all these gossipy girls, the cheerleaders. It's so cliquey." Still, she says she enjoys attending a regular school: "I love it cause it's the best of both worlds. I can go back and be a normal kid, play sports, and have fun."

—— " ——

Vega doesn't really talk about him, except that he isn't part of the family anymore: "I have four sisters and since my dad's not here anymore, we're all girls."

YOUTH AND EDUCATION

Vega was just four years old when her family moved from Florida to southern California. Her mother hoped to break into acting, and Alexa had an offer to audition for the sitcom "Full House." The move to Hollywood took so long that Alexa missed the audition. Instead, her mother found a job with a talent agency, a business that helps artists and performers find acting jobs. She soon realized that her precocious daughter had the talent to be an actress. Vega's first audition was successful, and she soon won a part on the TV series "Evening Shade" starring Burt Reynolds.

Because she spends a lot of time filming, Vega often gets tutored on the movie set. But when she's not making a movie, she attends a regular school. In 2003, Vega began tenth grade at Notre Dame Girls Catholic High School in Sherman Oaks, California. Despite her success as an actress, she still faces the same types of experiences at school that all kids face, some great and some not so great. She had this to say about her experiences in ninth grade: "To a certain extent it's wonderful but you still have all these gossipy girls, the cheerleaders. It's so cliquey." Still, she says she enjoys attending a regular school: "I love it cause it's the best of both worlds. I can go back and be a normal kid, play sports, and have fun." Her favorite subject is math, and she plans to attend college after she graduates from high school.

CAREER HIGHLIGHTS

Developing a Career in Television

Vega has been working in the entertainment business her whole life. She began her career at age five, when she landed the role of Emily Newton on the CBS series "Evening Shade." This series focused on Wood Newton, a football coach in small-town Arkansas, and his family and friends. Vega joined the cast as the Newtons' youngest daughter during the show's last season, from 1993 to 1994. During this first acting experience Vega was surrounded with well-known performers: Burt Reynolds and Marilu Henner played her parents, and Ossie Davis, Hal Holbrook, and Charles Durning were also regular cast members. After the series concluded, Vega made guest appearances on the hit medical dramas "ER" and "Chicago Hope." She also won small parts in two television movies, *It Was Him or Us* (1995) and *A Promise to Caroline* (1996). In both of these melodramas she appeared in flashbacks as a younger version of the main character.

In 1996 Vega returned to series television with a role in the ABC sitcom "Life's Work." This series followed the work and home lives of Lisa Hunter, a busy lawyer married to a basketball coach. Vega played Tess, the oldest of Lisa's two kids. The series didn't find a big audience and lasted only a single season. Vega had better luck with her next sitcom role, in the CBS series "Ladies Man." The show starred Alfred Molina as a furniture maker in a household full of women, including Vega as one of his daughters. This series lasted two full seasons, from 1999 to 2001, but wasn't a big hit.

As she grew older, however, Vega began finding bigger parts in television movies. In 2000 she appeared in *Run the Wild Fields*, a historical drama aired by the cable network Showtime. Vega played Pug, the tomboy daughter of a soldier missing in action during World War II. The film shows Pug and her mother struggling to run their farm alone until a young drifter lends them a hand. Vega had a large role in this film, in which she received third billing. In 2001 she had another significant role in the Hallmark Hall of Fame drama *Follow the Stars Home*. She played Amy, a girl who helps a neighbor woman with her disabled child. While Amy is a good-natured girl, she comes from an unstable home: her widowed mother drinks too much, and her mother's boyfriend is abusive. While the movie itself didn't get terrific reviews, one critic singled out Vega's excellent performance and noted that the young actress "is so winning that she makes a good case for building the movie around Amy."

Making a Mark in Hollywood

Vega's early career wasn't limited to just television. She had small parts in several movies, including *Little Giants* (1994) and *Nine Months* (1995). In both of these comedies she had a bit role as someone's daughter or little sister. In the 1996 film *Twister* she had a brief but memorable part as the

Vega appeared with Joanne Whalley and Sean Patrick Flanery in the Showtime historical drama Run the Wild Fields.

young version of Helen Hunt's tornado-chasing scientist, JoAnne. In the opening scene of the film we see young JoAnne, played by Vega, as she and her family hide from a deadly tornado. The scene required Vega to look terrified as her father is snatched away by fierce winds—a special effect that was added after she filmed her scene.

Vega continued her Hollywood career with a series of film roles where she played the daughter to some of Hollywood's biggest stars. In *The Glimmer Man* (1996), for instance, she played the daughter of action star Steven Seagal. That same year she played Alec Baldwin's daughter in the drama *Ghosts of Mississippi,* which was based on a true story. Baldwin stars as prosecutor Bobby DeLaughter, who re-opened a 25-year-old murder case against white supremacist Byron De La Beckwith. Beckwith shot black civil-rights activist Medgar Evers to death in 1963, but went free after two all-white juries failed to convict him. The film tells the story from the point-of-view of the prosecutor, including how his discoveries affect his relationships with his family. Many critics felt these family scenes detracted from the drama of the story, but they gave Vega valuable experience nonetheless.

In 1999, Vega co-starred as Michelle Pfeiffer's daughter in the film *The Deep End of the Ocean*. This family drama shows the devastating effects of a kidnaping on a Midwestern family, especially when the missing son is rediscovered after an absence of seven years. Vega played Kerry, the daughter who was only a baby when her brother went missing. She is confused when this complete stranger moves into her house and changes her family. The film received mixed reviews overall, but was praised for the believable family dynamics portrayed by Vega and her co-stars.

Despite working on big Hollywood films, Vega has tried to stay a normal, down-to-earth girl. Working on film sets meant that she was surrounded by adults—and adult language. So she developed a method of getting people to watch their language by charging cast and crew for each swear word said in her presence. "I collect a dollar for each dirty word I hear, five dollars for each use of one particularly dirty four-letter word," she explained. "During the filming of one movie . . . I collected a total of $700. I gave it to charity."

———— *"* ————

Working on film sets meant that Vega was surrounded by adults— and adult language. "I collect a dollar for each dirty word I hear, five dollars for each use of one particularly dirty four-letter word," she explained. "During the filming of one movie . . . I collected a total of $700. I gave it to charity."

———— *"* ————

Starring as a Spy Kid

Vega spent half a year auditioning and then training for her first starring role, as Carmen Cortez in *Spy Kids* (2001). Robert Rodriguez, the writer and director of the movie, originally thought Carmen's character should be younger than a preteen, but he decided to change the part after seeing Vega audition. "From the first time I saw her, I thought she was amazing," Rodriguez remarked. "You buy that she's strong, take-charge, and confident, that she can strap on a jet pack and rescue her brother." To prepare for her role, Vega dyed her blond hair dark brown and spent over a month in gymnastics training. She ended up performing most of her own stunts,

Vega admits that she and Daryl Sabara fought while making Spy Kids, *"but it was play-fighting, normal brother-sister stuff."*

including her favorite, a spectacular chase scene wearing a jet pack. "Every kid dreams of flying, and I got to do that." She also contributed one of the funniest one-liners in the film: Carmen's "Oh, shiitake mushrooms!" came from Vega's own experience — a phrase a crew member used to avoid paying one of her "cursing fines."

Vega plays Carmen Cortez, a normal 12-year-old girl with an irritating little brother (played by Daryl Sabara) and boring parents (played by Antonio Banderas and Carla Gugino). When her parents are kidnaped, Carmen discovers they had a secret life as OSS spies before they retired to raise their family. In fact, not only were they spies, they were among the greatest spies in history. Carmen and her brother, Juni, must spring into action to locate and rescue their mom and dad. Along the way they find a lost uncle, amazing gadgets, robotic children, a sinister television show host, and an evil lair that is more fun house than madhouse. Although there is plenty of action, in the end the film emphasizes the importance of families and sticking together.

Spy Kids was a surprise number one hit at the box office and earned over $112 million dollars in U.S. ticket sales. Critics and audiences alike were charmed by the film's mix of family togetherness, action adventure, and spy gadgets. Vega and Sabara's performance as bickering siblings was also praised for its realism. The two child actors first worked together in 1996 on the set of the series "Life's Work" and got along very well. Vega admitted that she and Sabara fought off the set, "but it was play-fighting, normal brother-sister stuff." Director Rodriguez became a father figure to her, and the family atmosphere on the set translated to the screen. The strong, loving, talented Latino family of *Spy Kids* is one of the things that Vega, who is half-Hispanic and fluent in Spanish, loves best about the movie.

Becoming a Full-Fledged Spy

No sooner had the first *Spy Kids* movie made its debut than Vega began working on its sequel, *Spy Kids 2: The Island of Lost Dreams* (2002). Having proven their abilities as spies, Carmen and Juni are now full-fledged members of the OSS spy organization. They attend a specialized spy school, use even cooler spy gadgets, and go out on assignments. The one thing that spoils their new life is competition from the irritating Gary and Gerti Giggles, who try to steal the spotlight from Carmen and Juni. The Cortez siblings' father, Gregorio, is also competing against Gary and Gerti's father, Donnagon Giggles, to become the new director of the OSS. But when the Giggles siblings manage to get Juni thrown out of the OSS, and Donnagon takes over the agency, Carmen and Juni strike back. They get the Giggles sent to the middle of the desert while they take on the prime assignment of recovering

Robert Rodriguez, the writer and director of Spy Kids, *originally thought Carmen's character should be younger than a preteen, but he decided to change the part after seeing Vega audition. "From the first time I saw her, I thought she was amazing," he remarked. "You buy that she's strong, take-charge, and confident, that she can strap on a jet pack and rescue her brother."*

a stolen piece of technology. The "transmooker" device prevents electronic tools from working and has the potential to destroy the world in the wrong hands.

Carmen and Juni's mission takes them to a mysterious island inhabited by strange, mutant creatures. These are strange cross-breed animals, from a spider monkey to horse flies and bull frogs. Carmen and Juni find their gadgets are useless on the island and they must use their intelligence to

Vega's standout performance in Spy Kids 2 *led a* New York Times *critic to write: "Forget Vin Diesel. For my money the multicultural action-movie star of the moment is Alexa Vega."*

succeed. Eventually they gain the help of the island's strange scientist to destroy the transmooker device and save the day. Not only do their parents give them an assist, but their retired spy grandparents, played by Ricardo Montalban and Holland Taylor, join in as well. Again, the film emphasizes the importance of family. Vega and Sabara continued to be believable as a brother and sister who bicker back and forth but are there for each other when trouble strikes.

In *Spy Kids 2* Vega showed new talents. The ending shows Carmen Cortez disguised as a singer, and Vega provided her own vocals for the scene. Her song also appeared on the *Spy Kids 2* soundtrack. Vega was able to expand the character of Carmen, showing her growing up a bit: she has a crush on the handsome Gary Giggles, even though she knows he's a sneak. The actress also had to use her imagination when filming scenes with the island's animals, including a fight scene against an army of skeletons. All these creatures were created using special effects after Vega shot the scenes. So she often acted in an empty space in front of a blank screen, so filmmakers could go back later and add the backgrounds and the rest of the scenery through special effects.

> —— " ——
>
> *Vega often acted in an empty space in front of a blank screen, so filmmakers could go back later and add the special effects. But she didn't mind the challenge. "We get to imagine these crazy, scary creatures. It makes it more fun and exciting to see the finished product and say, 'Ooh cool, that's what it looks like.'"*
>
> —— " ——

But Vega didn't mind the challenge. "We get to imagine these crazy, scary creatures. It makes it more fun and exciting to see the finished product and say, 'Ooh cool, that's what it looks like.'" Her standout performance in *Spy Kids 2* led a *New York Times* critic to write: "Forget Vin Diesel. For my money the multicultural action-movie star of the moment is Alexa Vega."

Finishing the Game

In 2003 Vega again appeared as Carmen Cortez in *Spy Kids 3-D: Game Over*. This film has Carmen working for the OSS and investigating a sinister video game designed to trap children's minds. As the film opens, Carmen has been lost inside the game; only her brother Juni, who has retired from the spy business, can save her. He enters the game, a computer-generated virtual world that the movie audience sees in three dimensions

(3-D) by using special glasses. After facing many challenges Juni catches up to Carmen on Level 4 of the game. The two of them then pursue the creator of the game, the evil Toymaker (played by Sylvester Stallone). They need to shut down the game and keep him from escaping. When he does escape, it is only with the help of all their family and friends that Carmen and Juni triumph.

Because much of the action in *Spy Kids 3-D* takes place in a video game, there were many more special effects shots than in the first two films. So Vega spent a lot of time in front of a blank screen pretending that she could see the scenery or creature that would be added later through special effects. Vega did her own stunts again in this film—her favorite was the scene where she surfs through a river of lava. "There was this contraption shaped like a really wide U; it looked like we were either on a skateboard or snowboard, and we had all these stunt guys pulling us back and forth. I thought it was going to be really weird going up there, and it was, but it was really cool because you really felt like you were up there surfing with all the wind blowing and hearing Robert [Rodriguez, the director] shout: 'there's a monster behind you!'"

> **Vega admits to crying during the last day of filming Spy Kids 3.** "It's sad because we've worked with everyone for four years, they've become like my family and they've seen me grow into a teenager. But it's been a wonderful experience, because Robert's given us a real boost and hopefully we can go far in our careers."

Vega sang again for the third *Spy Kids* soundtrack, and also got the chance to perform live before the *Spy Kids 3* premiere. She enjoyed it so much she is now thinking of including music in her career. "We were trying to practice everything on stage and it was kind of chaotic. But when it happened it was fun. When I finished I told my mom I wanted to be a rock star, because the rush you get on stage is so great."

Spy Kids 3: Game Over, as the title suggests, was the last of the series. Vega admits to crying during the last day of filming. "It's sad because we've worked with everyone for four years, they've become like my family and they've seen me grow into a teenager. But it's been a wonderful experience, because Robert's given us a real boost and hopefully we can go far in our careers." Vega is also looking forward to trying something new. After

Spy Kids 3 she noted that "I want to be able to move on and be good and be able to do different things."

Future Plans and Projects

Although the *Spy Kids* series is over, Vega has many plans for the future. In fall 2003 she began working on the movie *Sleepover.* In this comedy Vega plays a girl whose best friend is moving away the summer before they enter high school. She throws a slumber party for her friends on the same night that a group of popular girls are having their own get-together. The two groups of girls end up competing in a scavenger hunt, with the prize being the rights to the best lunch table at the high school. Vega also has a role in the upcoming drama *State's Evidence,* and she has considered making another television series as well.

Vega enjoys attending movie premieres, like this one for Freaky Friday.

Outside of acting, Vega is looking forward to continuing her education. After high school, she hopes to attend college some day. She would like to study film, and perhaps add writing and directing to her Hollywood résumé. She has already written film scripts and made her own home movies. "I have a lot of ideas, but the writing takes so long," she commented. "I'm serious about it, though." She is also thinking about turning her contributions to the *Spy Kids* soundtracks into a singing career. "When I grow up, I want to be an actress if not a director, or a writer or a singer. I can't decide. But I do want to go to college for other choices."

In the meantime, Vega doesn't mind being recognized by her fans. "It's kind of weird but I like it; I like making little kids happy." She hopes to live up to her fans' expectations, adding that it's "exciting that someone looks up to you so much. That's why you have to set a good example, make sure you're always being humble and grounded." Luckily for Vega, that's something she gets from her family. Her mother and little sisters remind her

—— " ——

Vega doesn't mind being recognized by her fans. "It's kind of weird but I like it; I like making little kids happy." She hopes to live up to her fans' expectations, adding that it's "exciting that someone looks up to you so much. That's why you have to set a good example, make sure you're always being humble and grounded."

—— " ——

she's just a normal kid. "My mom says if I let this all go to my head and misbehave she's going to flush my action figure down the toilet," Vega jokes. She and her *Spy Kids* co-stars are just like anyone else, she says: "We're not really movie stars; we're just in a movie."

FAVORITE MOVIES

Vega enjoys watching action movies like *Austin Powers* and *Mission Impossible*. Her favorite actress is Natalie Portman, who played Padme in *Star Wars 1: The Phantom Menace* and *Star Wars 2: Attack of the Clones*. Vega also admires Jodie Foster, a former child actor who grew up to become an Oscar-winning actress and director.

HOBBIES AND OTHER INTERESTS

Vega calls herself a tomboy. She enjoys fishing, gymnastics, and playing football and basketball (she once played point guard on a boys' basketball team). She also enjoys her family pets, which include a dog, cat, chickens, and hairless rats. Like many teenagers, she likes spending time with friends and hanging out at the mall. She also enjoys listening to music and dancing to hip-hop.

SELECTED CREDITS

Movie Roles

Little Giants, 1994
Nine Months, 1995
Twister, 1996
The Glimmer Man, 1996
Ghosts of Mississippi, 1996 (also released as *Ghosts from the Past*)
Dennis the Menace Strikes Again, 1998
The Deep End of the Ocean, 1999
NetForce, 1999
Spy Kids, 2001

Spy Kids 2: The Island of Lost Dreams, 2002
Spy Kids 3: Game Over, 2003

Television Movies and Series

"Evening Shade," 1993-94 (series)
It Was Him or Us, 1995 (movie)
"Life's Work," 1996 (series)
A Promise to Caroline, 1996 (movie),
Shattered Mind, 1996 (movie; also known as *The Terror Inside*)
"Ladies Man," 1999 (series)
Run the Wild Fields, 2000 (movie)
Follow the Stars Home, 2001 (movie)

FURTHER READING

Books

Contemporary Theatre, Film, and Television, Vol. 40, 2002

Periodicals

Boston Herald, Aug. 5, 2002, p.29
Dallas Morning News, Aug. 7, 2002, p.C1
Detroit News, Aug. 10, 2002, p.1
Houston Chronicle, Apr. 5, 2001, p.6
New York Times, Aug. 7, 2002, p.E6
Ottawa (Ontario) Sun, Mar. 30, 2001, p.33
People, Apr. 16, 2001, p.145
Tennessean, Apr. 4, 2001, p.D3
Vanity Fair, July, 2003, p.96
Washington Post, Mar. 30, 2001, p.C11

Online Articles

http://actionadventure.about.com/library/weekly/2001/aa033001a.htm
(*About.com,* "What You Need to Know About Action-Adventure Movies: Kids . . . *Spy Kids* — Alexa Vega and Daryl Sabara," 2001)
http://actionadventure.about.com/library/weekly/2002/aa032002.htm
(*About.com,* "What You Need to Know About Action-Adventure Movies: Exclusive Alexa Vega Interview," 2002)
http://www.bbc.co.uk/films/
(*BBC,* "Films — Interviews: Alexa Vega," July 30, 2003)

http://www.tribute.ca/?newsletter=95

(*Tribute Moviemail*, "Star Chat: An Interview with Alexa Vega," July 18, 2003)

Online Databases

Biography Resource Center Online, 2003, article from *Contemporary Theatre, Film, and Television,* 2002

ADDRESS

Alexa Vega
SDB Partners, Inc.
1801 Avenue of the Stars, Suite 902
Los Angeles, CA 90067

WORLD WIDE WEB SITES

http://www.spykids.com

Photo and Illustration Credits

Natalie Babbitt/Photo: Farrar, Straus and Giroux; copyright © Disney Enterprises, Inc. (p. 18). Covers: THE SEARCH FOR DELICIOUS copyright © 1969 by Natalie Babbitt; KNEEKNOCK RISE copyright © 1970 by Natalie Babbitt; TUCK EVERLASTING copyright © 1975 by Natalie Babbitt. Cover art copyright © 1975 by Natalie Babbitt; THE EYES OF AMARYLLIS copyright © 1977 by Natalie Babbitt, all Sunburst Books/Farrar, Straus and Giroux; PEACOCK AND OTHER POEMS (Farrar, Straus and Giroux) text copyright © 2002 by George Bahlke. Illustrations copyright © 2002 by Natalie Babbitt.

David Beckham/Photos: Steve Finn/Getty Images; Shaun Botterill/Getty Images (pp. 30, 33); Ross Kinnaird/Getty Images; AP/Wide World Photos; Stuart Franklin/Getty Images; AP/Wide World Photos.

Matel Dawson/Photos: AP/Wide World Photos (p. 45); Wayne State University; Ric Bielaczyc/Wayne State University.

Lisa Leslie/Photos: Andrew D. Bernstein/WNBAE/Getty Images; AP/Wide World Photos; Ken Levine/Getty Images; Doug Pensinger/Getty Images; Garrett Ellwood/WNBAE/Getty Images; Mike Blake/Reuters; AP/Wide World Photos; Jed Jacobsohn/Getty Images. Front cover: D. Clarke Evans/WNBAE/Getty Images.

Linkin Park/Photos: copyright © Joe Giron/CORBIS; copyright © Clay Patrick McBride/Retna; copyright © Jason Messer/Retna; Mike Blake/Reuters. CD covers: HYBRID THEORY copyright © 2000 Zomba Songs Inc.; METEORA © (P) 2003 Warner Bros. Records Inc.

Irene D. Long/Photos: NASA; copyright © Bettmann/CORBIS; NASA.

Mandy Moore/Photos: copyright © Paul Smith/Featureflash/Retna; Walt Disney Pictures/Getty Images (p. 113); copyright © 2003 Sophie Giraud/New Line Productions (p. 115). DVD cover: A WALK TO REMEMBER copyright © 2002 Pandora, Inc. Artwork and Photography copyright © 2002 Warner Bros. CD covers: SO REAL copyright © 1999 Sony Music Entertainment Inc./(P) 1999 Sony Music Entertainment Inc.; MANDY MOORE copyright © 2001 Sony Music Entertainment Inc./(P) 2001 Sony Music Entertainment Inc.; COVERAGE copyright © 2003 Sony Music

How to Use the Cumulative Index

Our indexes have a new look. In an effort to make our indexes easier to use, we've combined the Name and General Index into a new, Cumulative Index. This single ready-reference resource covers all the volumes in *Biography Today*, both the general series and the special subject series. The new Cumulative Index contains complete listings of all individuals who have appeared in *Biography Today* since the series began. Their names appear in bold-faced type, followed by the issue in which they appear. The Cumulative Index also includes references for the occupations, nationalities, and ethnic and minority origins of individuals profiled in *Biography Today*.

We have also made some changes to our specialty indexes, the Places of Birth Index and the Birthday Index. To consolidate and to save space, the Places of Birth Index and the Birthday Index will no longer appear in the January and April issues of the softbound subscription series. But these indexes can still be found in the September issue of the softbound subscription series, in the hardbound Annual Cumulation at the end of each year, and in each volume of the special subject series.

General Series

The General Series of *Biography Today* is denoted in the index with the month and year of the issue in which the individual appeared. Each individual also appears in the Annual Cumulation for that year.

Special Subject Series

The Special Subject Series of *Biography Today* are each denoted in the index with an abbreviated form of the series name, plus the number of the volume in which the individual appears. They are listed as follows.

Adams, Ansel . . . . Artist V.1   (Artists)
Card, Orson Scott . . . . Author V.14   (Authors)
Diaz, Cameron . . . . PerfArt V.3   (Performing Artists)
Kapell, Dave . . . . Science V.8   (Scientists & Inventors)
Milbrett, Tiffeny . . . . Sport V.10   (Sports)
Peterson, Roger Tory . . . . WorLdr V.1   (World Leaders:
    Environmental Leaders)
Sadat, Anwar . . . . WorLdr V.2   (World Leaders:
    Modern African Leaders)
Wolf, Hazel . . . . WorLdr V.3   (World Leaders:
    Environmental Leaders 2)

Updates

Updated information on selected individuals appears in the Appendix at the end of some issues of the *Biography Today* Annual Cumulation. In the index, the original entry is listed first, followed by any updates.

Arafat, Yasir . . . . Sep 94; Update 94;
    Update 95; Update 96; Update 97; Update 98;
    Update 00; Update 01; Update 02
Gates, Bill . . . . Apr 93; Update 98;
    Update 00; Science V.5; Update 01
Griffith Joyner, Florence . . . . Sport V.1;
    Update 98
Sanders, Barry . . . . Sep 95; Update 99
Spock, Dr. Benjamin . . . . Sep 95; Update 98
Yeltsin, Boris . . . . Apr 92; Update 93;
    Update 95; Update 96; Update 98; Update 00

Cumulative Index

This cumulative index includes names, occupations, nationalities, and ethnic and minority origins that pertain to all individuals profiled in *Biography Today* since the debut of the series in 1992.

CUMULATIVE INDEX

Biography Today

General Series

For ages 9 and above

"*Biography Today* will be useful in elementary and middle school libraries and in public library children's collections where there is a need for biographies of current personalities. High schools serving reluctant readers may also want to consider a subscription."
— *Booklist,* American Library Association

"Highly recommended for the young adult audience. Readers will delight in the accessible, energetic, tell-all style; teachers, librarians, and parents will welcome the clever format, intelligent and informative text. It should prove especially useful in motivating 'reluctant' readers or literate nonreaders."
— *MultiCultural Review*

"Written in a friendly, almost chatty tone, the profiles offer quick, objective information. While coverage of current figures makes *Biography Today* a useful reference tool, an appealing format and wide scope make it a fun resource to browse." — *School Library Journal*

"The best source for current information at a level kids can understand."
— Kelly Bryant, School Librarian, Carlton, OR

"Easy for kids to read. We love it! Don't want to be without it."
— Lynn McWhirter, School Librarian, Rockford, IL

Biography Today **General Series** includes a unique combination of current biographical profiles that teachers and librarians — and the readers themselves — tell us are most appealing. The **General Series** is available as a 3-issue subscription; hardcover annual cumulation; or subscription plus cumulation.

Within the **General Series**, your readers will find a variety of sketches about:

- Authors
- Musicians
- Political leaders
- Sports figures
- Movie actresses & actors
- Cartoonists
- Scientists
- Astronauts
- TV personalities
- and the movers & shakers in many other fields!

ONE-YEAR SUBSCRIPTION
- 3 softcover issues, 6" x 9"
- Published in January, April, and September
- 1-year subscription, $60
- 150 pages per issue
- 10 profiles per issue
- Contact sources for additional information
- Cumulative General, Places of Birth, and Birthday Indexes

HARDBOUND ANNUAL CUMULATION
- Sturdy 6" x 9" hardbound volume
- Published in December
- $62 per volume
- 450 pages per volume
- 25-30 profiles — includes all profiles found in softcover issues for that calendar year
- Cumulative General, Places of Birth, and Birthday Indexes
- Special appendix features current updates of previous profiles

SUBSCRIPTION AND CUMULATION COMBINATION
- $99 for 3 softcover issues plus the hardbound volume

223

1992

Paula Abdul
Andre Agassi
Kirstie Alley
Terry Anderson
Roseanne Arnold
Isaac Asimov
James Baker
Charles Barkley
Larry Bird
Judy Blume
Berke Breathed
Garth Brooks
Barbara Bush
George Bush
Fidel Castro
Bill Clinton
Bill Cosby
Diana, Princess of Wales
Shannen Doherty
Elizabeth Dole
David Duke
Gloria Estefan
Mikhail Gorbachev
Steffi Graf
Wayne Gretzky
Matt Groening
Alex Haley
Hammer
Martin Handford
Stephen Hawking
Hulk Hogan
Saddam Hussein
Lee Iacocca
Bo Jackson
Mae Jemison
Peter Jennings
Steven Jobs
Pope John Paul II
Magic Johnson
Michael Jordon
Jackie Joyner-Kersee
Spike Lee
Mario Lemieux
Madeleine L'Engle
Jay Leno
Yo-Yo Ma
Nelson Mandela
Wynton Marsalis
Thurgood Marshall
Ann Martin
Barbara McClintock
Emily Arnold McCully
Antonia Novello

Sandra Day O'Connor
Rosa Parks
Jane Pauley
H. Ross Perot
Luke Perry
Scottie Pippen
Colin Powell
Jason Priestley
Queen Latifah
Yitzhak Rabin
Sally Ride
Pete Rose
Nolan Ryan
H. Norman
    Schwarzkopf
Jerry Seinfeld
Dr. Seuss
Gloria Steinem
Clarence Thomas
Chris Van Allsburg
Cynthia Voigt
Bill Watterson
Robin Williams
Oprah Winfrey
Kristi Yamaguchi
Boris Yeltsin

1993

Maya Angelou
Arthur Ashe
Avi
Kathleen Battle
Candice Bergen
Boutros Boutros-Ghali
Chris Burke
Dana Carvey
Cesar Chavez
Henry Cisneros
Hillary Rodham Clinton
Jacques Cousteau
Cindy Crawford
Macaulay Culkin
Lois Duncan
Marian Wright Edelman
Cecil Fielder
Bill Gates
Sara Gilbert
Dizzy Gillespie
Al Gore
Cathy Guisewite
Jasmine Guy
Anita Hill
Ice-T
Darci Kistler

k.d. lang
Dan Marino
Rigoberta Menchu
Walter Dean Myers
Martina Navratilova
Phyllis Reynolds Naylor
Rudolf Nureyev
Shaquille O'Neal
Janet Reno
Jerry Rice
Mary Robinson
Winona Ryder
Jerry Spinelli
Denzel Washington
Keenen Ivory Wayans
Dave Winfield

1994

Tim Allen
Marian Anderson
Mario Andretti
Ned Andrews
Yasir Arafat
Bruce Babbitt
Mayim Bialik
Bonnie Blair
Ed Bradley
John Candy
Mary Chapin Carpenter
Benjamin Chavis
Connie Chung
Beverly Cleary
Kurt Cobain
F.W. de Klerk
Rita Dove
Linda Ellerbee
Sergei Fedorov
Zlata Filipovic
Daisy Fuentes
Ruth Bader Ginsburg
Whoopi Goldberg
Tonya Harding
Melissa Joan Hart
Geoff Hooper
Whitney Houston
Dan Jansen
Nancy Kerrigan
Alexi Lalas
Charlotte Lopez
Wilma Mankiller
Shannon Miller
Toni Morrison
Richard Nixon
Greg Norman
Severo Ochoa

River Phoenix
Elizabeth Pine
Jonas Salk
Richard Scarry
Emmitt Smith
Will Smith
Steven Spielberg
Patrick Stewart
R.L. Stine
Lewis Thomas
Barbara Walters
Charlie Ward
Steve Young
Kim Zmeskal

1995

Troy Aikman
Jean-Bertrand Aristide
Oksana Baiul
Halle Berry
Benazir Bhutto
Jonathan Brandis
Warren E. Burger
Ken Burns
Candace Cameron
Jimmy Carter
Agnes de Mille
Placido Domingo
Janet Evans
Patrick Ewing
Newt Gingrich
John Goodman
Amy Grant
Jesse Jackson
James Earl Jones
Julie Krone
David Letterman
Rush Limbaugh
Heather Locklear
Reba McEntire
Joe Montana
Cosmas Ndeti
Hakeem Olajuwon
Ashley Olsen
Mary-Kate Olsen
Jennifer Parkinson
Linus Pauling
Itzhak Perlman
Cokie Roberts
Wilma Rudolph
Salt 'N' Pepa
Barry Sanders
William Shatner
Elizabeth George
    Speare

Dr. Benjamin Spock
Jonathan Taylor
　Thomas
Vicki Van Meter
Heather Whitestone
Pedro Zamora

1996

Aung San Suu Kyi
Boyz II Men
Brandy
Ron Brown
Mariah Carey
Jim Carrey
Larry Champagne III
Christo
Chelsea Clinton
Coolio
Bob Dole
David Duchovny
Debbi Fields
Chris Galeczka
Jerry Garcia
Jennie Garth
Wendy Guey
Tom Hanks
Alison Hargreaves
Sir Edmund Hillary
Judith Jamison
Barbara Jordan
Annie Leibovitz
Carl Lewis
Jim Lovell
Mickey Mantle
Lynn Margulis
Iqbal Masih
Mark Messier
Larisa Oleynik
Christopher Pike
David Robinson
Dennis Rodman
Selena
Monica Seles
Don Shula
Kerri Strug
Tiffani-Amber Thiessen
Dave Thomas
Jaleel White

1997

Madeleine Albright
Marcus Allen
Gillian Anderson
Rachel Blanchard
Zachery Ty Bryan
Adam Ezra Cohen
Claire Danes
Celine Dion
Jean Driscoll
Louis Farrakhan
Ella Fitzgerald
Harrison Ford
Bryant Gumbel
John Johnson
Michael Johnson
Maya Lin
George Lucas
John Madden
Bill Monroe
Alanis Morissette
Sam Morrison
Rosie O'Donnell
Muammar el-Qaddafi
Christopher Reeve
Pete Sampras
Pat Schroeder
Rebecca Sealfon
Tupac Shakur
Tabitha Soren
Herbert Tarvin
Merlin Tuttle
Mara Wilson

1998

Bella Abzug
Kofi Annan
Neve Campbell
Sean Combs (Puff
　Daddy)
Dalai Lama (Tenzin
　Gyatso)
Diana, Princess of Wales
Leonardo DiCaprio
Walter E. Diemer
Ruth Handler
Hanson
Livan Hernandez
Jewel
Jimmy Johnson
Tara Lipinski
Jody-Anne Maxwell
Dominique Moceanu
Alexandra Nechita

Brad Pitt
LeAnn Rimes
Emily Rosa
David Satcher
Betty Shabazz
Kordell Stewart
Shinichi Suzuki
Mother Teresa
Mike Vernon
Reggie White
Kate Winslet

1999

Ben Affleck
Jennifer Aniston
Maurice Ashley
Kobe Bryant
Bessie Delany
Sadie Delany
Sharon Draper
Sarah Michelle Gellar
John Glenn
Savion Glover
Jeff Gordon
David Hampton
Lauryn Hill
King Hussein
Lynn Johnston
Shari Lewis
Oseola McCarty
Mark McGwire
Slobodan Milosevic
Natalie Portman
J. K. Rowling
Frank Sinatra
Gene Siskel
Sammy Sosa
John Stanford
Natalia Toro
Shania Twain
Mitsuko Uchida
Jesse Ventura
Venus Williams

2000

Christina Aguilera
K.A. Applegate
Lance Armstrong
Backstreet Boys
Daisy Bates
Harry Blackmun
George W. Bush
Carson Daly
Ron Dayne
Henry Louis Gates, Jr.
Doris Haddock
　(Granny D)
Jennifer Love Hewitt
Chamique Holdsclaw
Katie Holmes
Charlayne Hunter-Gault
Johanna Johnson
Craig Kielburger
John Lasseter
Peyton Manning
Ricky Martin
John McCain
Walter Payton
Freddie Prinze, Jr.
Viviana Risca
Briana Scurry
George Thampy
CeCe Winans

2001

Jessica Alba
Christiane Amanpour
Drew Barrymore
Jeff Bezos
Destiny's Child
Dale Earnhardt
Carly Fiorina
Aretha Franklin
Cathy Freeman
Tony Hawk
Faith Hill
Kim Dae-jung
Madeleine L'Engle
Mariangela Lisanti
Frankie Muniz
*N Sync
Ellen Ochoa
Jeff Probst
Julia Roberts
Carl T. Rowan
Britney Spears
Chris Tucker
Lloyd D. Ward
Alan Webb
Chris Weinke

2002

Aaliyah
Osama bin Laden
Mary J. Blige
Aubyn Burnside
Aaron Carter
Julz Chavez
Dick Cheney
Hilary Duff
Billy Gilman
Rudolph Giuliani
Brian Griese
Jennifer Lopez
Dave Mirra
Dineh Mohajer
Leanne Nakamura
Daniel Radcliffe
Condoleezza Rice
Marla Runyan
Ruth Simmons
Mattie Stepanek
J.R.R. Tolkien
Barry Watson
Tyrone Willingham
Elijah Wood

2003

Yolanda Adams
Olivia Bennett
Mildred Benson
Alexis Bledel
Barry Bonds
Vincent Brooks
Laura Bush
Amanda Bynes
Kelly Clarkson
Vin Diesel
Eminem
Michele Forman
Vicente Fox
Millard Fuller
Josh Hartnett
Dolores Huerta
Sarah Hughes
Enrique Iglesias
Jeanette Lee
John Lewis
Nicklas Lidstrom
Clint Mathis
Donovan McNabb

Nelly
Andy Roddick
Gwen Stefani
Emma Watson
Meg Whitman
Reese Witherspoon
Yao Ming

2004

Natalie Babbitt
David Beckham
Matel Dawson, Jr.
Lisa Leslie
Linkin Park
Irene D. Long
Mandy Moore
Thich Nhat Hanh
Keanu Reeves
Alexa Vega

Biography Today

Subject Series

For ages 9 and above

Expands and complements the General Series and targets specific subject areas . . .

Our readers asked for it! They wanted more biographies, and the *Biography Today* Subject Series is our response to that demand. Now your readers can choose their special areas of interest and go on to read about their favorites in those fields. Priced at just $39 per volume, the following specific volumes are included in the *Biography Today* Subject Series:

- **Artists**
- **Authors**
- **Performing Artists**
- **Scientists & Inventors**
- **Sports**
- **World Leaders**
  Environmental Leaders
  Modern African Leaders

FEATURES AND FORMAT

- Sturdy 6" x 9" hardbound volumes
- Individual volumes, $39 each
- 200 pages per volume
- 10 profiles per volume — targets individuals within a specific subject area
- Contact sources for additional information
- Cumulative General, Places of Birth, and Birthday Indexes

NOTE: There is *no duplication of entries* between the **General Series** of *Biography Today* and the **Subject Series.**

AUTHORS

"A useful tool for children's assignment needs." — *School Library Journal*

"The prose is workmanlike: report writers will find enough detail to begin sound investigations, and browsers are likely to find someone of interest." — *School Library Journal*

SCIENTISTS & INVENTORS

"The articles are readable, attractively laid out, and touch on important points that will suit assignment needs. Browsers will note the clear writing and interesting details." — *School Library Journal*

"The book is excellent for demonstrating that scientists are real people with widely diverse backgrounds and personal interests. The biographies are fascinating to read." — *The Science Teacher*

SPORTS

"This series should become a standard resource in libraries that serve intermediate students." — *School Library Journal*

ENVIRONMENTAL LEADERS #1

"A tremendous book that fills a gap in the biographical category of books. This is a great reference book." — *Science Scope*

Artists

VOLUME 1

Ansel Adams
Romare Bearden
Margaret Bourke-White
Alexander Calder
Marc Chagall
Helen Frankenthaler
Jasper Johns
Jacob Lawrence
Henry Moore
Grandma Moses
Louise Nevelson
Georgia O'Keeffe
Gordon Parks
I.M. Pei
Diego Rivera
Norman Rockwell
Andy Warhol
Frank Lloyd Wright

Authors

VOLUME 1

Eric Carle
Alice Childress
Robert Cormier
Roald Dahl
Jim Davis
John Grisham
Virginia Hamilton
James Herriot
S.E. Hinton
M.E. Kerr
Stephen King
Gary Larson
Joan Lowery Nixon
Gary Paulsen
Cynthia Rylant
Mildred D. Taylor
Kurt Vonnegut, Jr.
E.B. White
Paul Zindel

VOLUME 2

James Baldwin
Stan and Jan Berenstain
David Macaulay
Patricia MacLachlan
Scott O'Dell
Jerry Pinkney
Jack Prelutsky

Lynn Reid Banks
Faith Ringgold
J.D. Salinger
Charles Schulz
Maurice Sendak
P.L. Travers
Garth Williams

VOLUME 3

Candy Dawson Boyd
Ray Bradbury
Gwendolyn Brooks
Ralph W. Ellison
Louise Fitzhugh
Jean Craighead George
E.L. Konigsburg
C.S. Lewis
Fredrick L. McKissack
Patricia C. McKissack
Katherine Paterson
Anne Rice
Shel Silverstein
Laura Ingalls Wilder

VOLUME 4

Betsy Byars
Chris Carter
Caroline B. Cooney
Christopher Paul Curtis
Anne Frank
Robert Heinlein
Marguerite Henry
Lois Lowry
Melissa Mathison
Bill Peet
August Wilson

VOLUME 5

Sharon Creech
Michael Crichton
Karen Cushman
Tomie dePaola
Lorraine Hansberry
Karen Hesse
Brian Jacques
Gary Soto
Richard Wright
Laurence Yep

VOLUME 6

Lloyd Alexander
Paula Danziger
Nancy Farmer
Zora Neale Hurston

Shirley Jackson
Angela Johnson
Jon Krakauer
Leo Lionni
Francine Pascal
Louis Sachar
Kevin Williamson

VOLUME 7

William H. Armstrong
Patricia Reilly Giff
Langston Hughes
Stan Lee
Julius Lester
Robert Pinsky
Todd Strasser
Jacqueline Woodson
Patricia C. Wrede
Jane Yolen

VOLUME 8

Amelia Atwater-Rhodes
Barbara Cooney
Paul Laurence Dunbar
Ursula K. Le Guin
Farley Mowat
Naomi Shihab Nye
Daniel Pinkwater
Beatrix Potter
Ann Rinaldi

VOLUME 9

Robb Armstrong
Cherie Bennett
Bruce Coville
Rosa Guy
Harper Lee
Irene Gut Opdyke
Philip Pullman
Jon Scieszka
Amy Tan
Joss Whedon

VOLUME 10

David Almond
Joan Bauer
Kate DiCamillo
Jack Gantos
Aaron McGruder
Richard Peck
Andrea Davis Pinkney
Louise Rennison
David Small
Katie Tarbox

VOLUME 11

Laurie Halse Anderson
Bryan Collier
Margaret Peterson
  Haddix
Milton Meltzer
William Sleator
Sonya Sones
Genndy Tartakovsky
Wendelin Van Draanen
Ruth White

VOLUME 12

An Na
Claude Brown
Meg Cabot
Virginia Hamilton
Chuck Jones
Robert Lipsyte
Lillian Morrison
Linda Sue Park
Pam Muñoz Ryan
Lemony Snicket
  (Daniel Handler)

VOLUME 13

Andrew Clements
Eoin Colfer
Sharon Flake
Edward Gorey
Francisco Jiménez
Astrid Lindgren
Chris Lynch
Marilyn Nelson
Tamora Pierce
Virginia Euwer Wolff

VOLUME 14

Orson Scott Card
Russell Freedman
Mary GrandPré
Dan Greenburg
Nikki Grimes
Laura Hillenbrand
Stephen Hillenburg
Norton Juster
Lurlene McDaniel
Stephanie S. Tolan

Performing Artists

VOLUME 1

Jackie Chan
Dixie Chicks
Kirsten Dunst
Suzanne Farrell
Bernie Mac
Shakira
Isaac Stern
Julie Taymor
Usher
Christina Vidal

VOLUME 2

Ashanti
Tyra Banks
Peter Jackson
Norah Jones
Quincy Jones
Avril Lavigne
George López
Marcel Marceau
Eddie Murphy
Julia Stiles

VOLUME 3

Michelle Branch
Cameron Diaz
Missy Elliott
Evelyn Glennie
Benji Madden
Joel Madden
Mike Myers
Fred Rogers
Twyla Tharp
Tom Welling
Yuen Wo-Ping

Scientists & Inventors

VOLUME 1

John Bardeen
Sylvia Earle
Dian Fossey
Jane Goodall
Bernadine Healy
Jack Horner
Mathilde Krim
Edwin Land
Louise & Mary Leakey
Rita Levi-Montalcini
J. Robert Oppenheimer
Albert Sabin
Carl Sagan
James D. Watson

VOLUME 2

Jane Brody
Seymour Cray
Paul Erdös
Walter Gilbert
Stephen Jay Gould
Shirley Ann Jackson
Raymond Kurzweil
Shannon Lucid
Margaret Mead
Garrett Morgan
Bill Nye
Eloy Rodriguez
An Wang

VOLUME 3

Luis W. Alvarez
Hans A. Bethe
Gro Harlem Brundtland
Mary S. Calderone
Ioana Dumitriu
Temple Grandin
John Langston
   Gwaltney
Bernard Harris
Jerome Lemelson
Susan Love
Ruth Patrick
Oliver Sacks
Richie Stachowski

VOLUME 4

David Attenborough
Robert Ballard
Ben Carson

Eileen Collins
Biruté Galdikas
Lonnie Johnson
Meg Lowman
Forrest Mars Sr.
Akio Morita
Janese Swanson

VOLUME 5

Steve Case
Douglas Engelbart
Shawn Fanning
Sarah Flannery
Bill Gates
Laura Groppe
Grace Murray Hopper
Steven Jobs
Rand and Robyn Miller
Shigeru Miyamoto
Steve Wozniak

VOLUME 6

Hazel Barton
Alexa Canady
Arthur Caplan
Francis Collins
Gertrude Elion
Henry Heimlich
David Ho
Kenneth Kamler
Lucy Spelman
Lydia Villa-Komaroff

VOLUME 7

Tim Berners-Lee
France Córdova
Anthony S. Fauci
Sue Hendrickson
Steve Irwin
John Forbes Nash, Jr.
Jerri Nielsen
Ryan Patterson
Nina Vasan
Gloria WilderBrathwaite

VOLUME 8

Deborah Blum
Richard Carmona
Helene Gayle
Dave Kapell
Adriana C. Ocampo
John Romero
Jamie Rubin
Jill Tarter
Earl Warrick
Edward O. Wilson

Sports

VOLUME 1

Hank Aaron
Kareem Abdul-Jabbar
Hassiba Boulmerka
Susan Butcher
Beth Daniel
Chris Evert
Ken Griffey, Jr.
Florence Griffith Joyner
Grant Hill
Greg LeMond
Pelé
Uta Pippig
Cal Ripken, Jr.
Arantxa Sanchez
   Vicario
Deion Sanders
Tiger Woods

VOLUME 2

Muhammad Ali
Donovan Bailey
Gail Devers
John Elway
Brett Favre
Mia Hamm
Anfernee "Penny"
   Hardaway
Martina Hingis
Gordie Howe
Jack Nicklaus
Richard Petty
Dot Richardson
Sheryl Swoopes
Steve Yzerman

VOLUME 3

Joe Dumars
Jim Harbaugh
Dominik Hasek
Michelle Kwan
Rebecca Lobo
Greg Maddux
Fatuma Roba
Jackie Robinson
John Stockton
Picabo Street
Pat Summitt
Amy Van Dyken

VOLUME 4

Wilt Chamberlain
Brandi Chastain
Derek Jeter
Karch Kiraly
Alex Lowe
Randy Moss
Se Ri Pak
Dawn Riley
Karen Smyers
Kurt Warner
Serena Williams

VOLUME 5

Vince Carter
Lindsay Davenport
Lisa Fernandez
Fu Mingxia
Jaromir Jagr
Marion Jones
Pedro Martinez
Warren Sapp
Jenny Thompson
Karrie Webb

VOLUME 6

Jennifer Capriati
Stacy Dragila
Kevin Garnett
Eddie George
Alex Rodriguez
Joe Sakic
Annika Sorenstam
Jackie Stiles
Tiger Woods
Aliy Zirkle

VOLUME 7

Tom Brady
Tara Dakides
Alison Dunlap
Sergio Garcia
Allen Iverson
Shirley Muldowney
Ty Murray
Patrick Roy
Tasha Schwiker

VOLUME 8

Simon Ammann
Shannon Bahrke
Kelly Clark
Vonetta Flowers
Cammi Granato
Chris Klug
Jonny Moseley
Apolo Ohno
Sylke Otto
Ryne Sanborn
Jim Shea, Jr.

VOLUME 9

Tori Allen
Layne Beachley
Sue Bird
Fabiola da Silva
Randy Johnson
Jason Kidd
Tony Stewart
Michael Vick
Ted Williams
Jay Yelas

VOLUME 10

Ryan Boyle
Natalie Coughlin
Allyson Felix
Dallas Friday
Jean-Sébastien Giguère
Phil Jackson
Keyshawn Johnson
Tiffeny Milbrett
Alfonso Soriano
Diana Taurasi

World Leaders

VOLUME 1: Environmental Leaders 1

Edward Abbey
Renee Askins
David Brower
Rachel Carson
Marjory Stoneman
  Douglas
Dave Foreman
Lois Gibbs
Wangari Maathai
Chico Mendes
Russell A. Mittermeier
Margaret and Olaus J.
  Murie
Patsy Ruth Oliver
Roger Tory Peterson
Ken Saro-Wiwa
Paul Watson
Adam Werbach

VOLUME 2: Modern African Leaders

Mohammed Farah
  Aidid
Idi Amin
Hastings Kamuzu Banda
Haile Selassie
Hassan II
Kenneth Kaunda
Jomo Kenyatta
Winnie Mandela
Mobutu Sese Seko
Robert Mugabe
Kwame Nkrumah
Julius Kambarage
  Nyerere
Anwar Sadat
Jonas Savimbi
Léopold Sédar Senghor
William V. S. Tubman

VOLUME 3: Environmental Leaders 2

John Cronin
Dai Qing
Ka Hsaw Wa
Winona LaDuke
Aldo Leopold
Bernard Martin
Cynthia Moss
John Muir
Gaylord Nelson
Douglas Tompkins
Hazel Wolf

Order Annual Sets of *Biography Today* and Save 20% Off the Regular Price!

Now, you can save time and money by purchasing *Biography Today* in Annual Sets! Save 20% off the regular price and get every single biography we publish in a year. Billed upon publication of the first volume, subsequent volumes are shipped throughout the year upon publication. Keep your *Biography Today* library current and complete with Annual Sets!

Place a standing order for annual sets and receive an additional 10% off!

Regular
price $473
**2004 Annual
Set $378**
You Save
$95

Biography Today 2004 Annual Set

13 volumes. 0-7808-0731-6. Annual set, $378. Includes:

2004 subscription (3 softcover issues)
2004 Hardbound Annual
Authors, Vol. 15 and Vol. 16
Business Leaders, Vol. 1
Performing Artists, Vol. 3 and Vol. 4
Scientists & Inventors, Vol. 9 and Vol. 10
Sports, Vol. 11 and Vol. 12

Regular
price $395
**2003 Annual
Set $316**
You Save
$79

Biography Today 2003 Annual Set

11 volumes. 0-7808-0730-8. Annual set, $316. Includes:

2003 subscription (3 softcover issues)
2003 Hardbound Annual
Authors, Vol. 13 and Vol. 14
Performing Artists, Vol. 1 and Vol. 2
Scientists & Inventors, Vol. 8
Sports, Vol. 9 and Vol. 10

Regular
price $297
**2002 Annual
Set $237**
You save
$60

Biography Today 2002 Annual Set

7 volumes. 0-7808-0729-4. Annual set, $237. Includes:

2002 Hardbound Annual
Authors, Vol. 11 and Vol. 12
Scientists & Inventors, Vol. 6 and Vol. 7
Sports, Vol. 7 and Vol. 8